# REFLECT
## LISTENING & SPEAKING

### JONATHAN BYGRAVE

**NATIONAL GEOGRAPHIC**
LEARNING

Australia · Brazil · Mexico · Singapore · United Kingdom · United States

National Geographic Learning,
a Cengage Company

**Reflect 2 Listening & Speaking**
Author: Jonathan Bygrave

Publisher: Sherrise Roehr
Executive Editor: Laura Le Dréan
Managing Editor: Jennifer Monaghan
Director of Global Marketing: Ian Martin
Product Marketing Manager: Tracy Baillie
Senior Content Project Manager: Mark Rzeszutek
Media Researcher: Stephanie Eenigenburg
Art Director: Brenda Carmichael
Senior Designer: Lisa Trager
Operations Coordinator: Hayley Chwazik-Gee
Manufacturing Buyer: Mary Beth Hennebury
Composition: MPS Limited

For permission to use material from this text or product, submit all requests online at **cengage.com/permissions**
Further permissions questions can be emailed to **permissionrequest@cengage.com**

Student Book ISBN: 978-0-357-44912-7
Student Book with Online Practice: 978-0-357-44918-9

**National Geographic Learning**
200 Pier 4 Boulevard
Boston, MA 02210

Locate your local office at **international.cengage.com/region**

Visit National Geographic Learning online at **ELTNGL.com**
Visit our corporate website at **www.cengage.com**

Printed in China
Print Number: 01       Print Year: 2021

# SCOPE AND SEQUENCE

 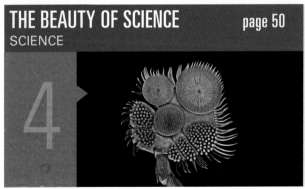

| SPEAKING & PRONUNCIATION | GRAMMAR | CRITICAL THINKING | REFLECT ACTIVITIES |
|---|---|---|---|
| Give opinions<br><br>Sounds and syllables | Quantifiers | Analyze what you know and don't know | ▶ Reflect on your neighborhood<br>▶ Give reasons for choosing your neighborhood<br>▶ Imagine life in Longyearbyen<br>▶ **UNIT TASK** Present advantages and disadvantages of your neighborhood |
| Ask for and give advice<br><br>The schwa /ə/ | Comparative and superlative adjectives | Evaluate information | ▶ Generate ideas about sibling behavior<br>▶ Compare yourself to siblings or friends<br>▶ Relate ideas to your experiences<br>▶ **UNIT TASK** Give a presentation about siblings |
| Make and respond to suggestions<br><br>Word stress | Question forms | Recognize reliable research | ▶ Discuss your experiences with music<br>▶ Make a playlist<br>▶ Evaluate a music survey<br>▶ **UNIT TASK** Present the results of a survey |
| Explain results<br><br>*-ed endings* | Simple past | Consider more than one cause | ▶ Understand steps in research<br>▶ Discuss a personal experiment<br>▶ Describe a home science experiment<br>▶ **UNIT TASK** Present the results of a science experiment |

| SPEAKING & PRONUNCIATION | GRAMMAR | CRITICAL THINKING | REFLECT ACTIVITIES |
|---|---|---|---|
| Give tips<br><br>Rhythm and stress | Present continuous | Analyze and evaluate advice | ▶ Consider your spending habits<br>▶ Discuss how social media impacts your spending<br>▶ Evaluate your money skills<br>▶ **UNIT TASK** Present a video giving tips |
| Explain purpose<br><br>Saying structure words | Adjectives and adverbs of manner | Categorize information | ▶ Analyze differences between animals<br>▶ Relate ideas to your life<br>▶ Categorize information about adaptation<br>▶ **UNIT TASK** Give a presentation on how to adapt |
| Ask follow-up questions<br><br>Connected speech | Present perfect | Use your imagination | ▶ Consider your future path<br>▶ Talk about a goal you reached<br>▶ Look for reasons behind results<br>▶ **UNIT TASK** Discover your perfect job |
| Ask questions to engage your audience<br><br>Intonation in questions | Future: *will* and *be going to* | Understand graphs | ▶ Discuss facts about the brain<br>▶ Ask questions about the brain<br>▶ Read a graph about happiness<br>▶ **UNIT TASK** Present an experiment on happiness |

# CONNECT TO IDEAS

***Reflect Listening & Speaking*** features relevant, global content to engage students while helping them acquire the academic language and skills they need. Specially-designed activities give students the opportunity to reflect on and connect ideas and language to their academic, work, and personal lives.

**National Geographic photography and content** invite students to investigate the world and discuss high-interest topics.

**Watch & Speak** and **Listen & Speak** sections center on high-interest video and audio that students will want to talk about as they build academic listening and speaking skills.

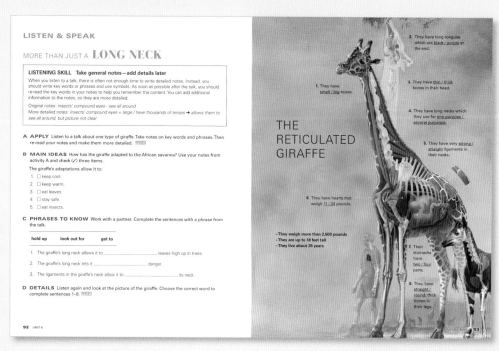

# CONNECT TO ACADEMIC SKILLS

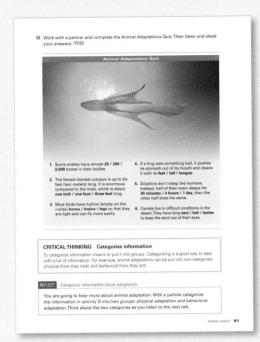

D Work with a partner and complete the Animal Adaptations Quiz. Then listen and check your answers.

**Animal Adaptations Quiz**

1. Some snakes have almost **20 / 200 / 2,000** bones in their bodies.

2. The female blanket octopus is up to six feet (two meters) long. It is enormous compared to the male, which is about **one inch / one foot / three feet** long.

3. Most birds have hollow (empty on the inside) **bones / brains / legs** so that they are light and can fly more easily.

4. If a frog eats something bad, it pushes its stomach out of its mouth and cleans it with its **feet / tail / tongue**.

5. Dolphins don't sleep like humans. Instead, half of their brain sleeps for **30 minutes / 4 hours / 1 day**, then the other half does the same.

6. Camels live in difficult conditions in the desert. They have long **ears / hair / lashes** to keep the sand out of their eyes.

**CRITICAL THINKING  Categorize information**
To categorize information means to put it into groups. Categorizing is a good way to deal with a lot of information. For example, animal adaptations can be put into two categories: *physical* (how they look) and *behavioral* (how they act).

**REFLECT**  Categorize information about adaptation

You are going to hear more about animal adaptation. With a partner categorize the information in activity D into two groups: physical adaptation and behavioral adaptation. Think about the two categories as you listen to the next talk.

ANIMAL MAGIC **91**

**Scaffolded activities** build confidence and provide students with a clear path to achieving final outcomes.

**Reflect activities** give students the opportunity to think critically about what they are learning and check their understanding.

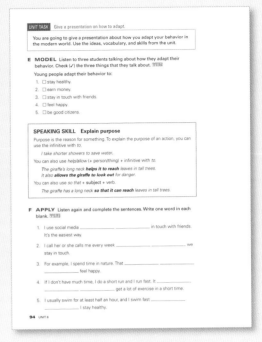

**UNIT TASK**  Give a presentation on how to adapt.

You are going to give a presentation about how you adapt your behavior in the modern world. Use the ideas, vocabulary, and skills from the unit.

E **MODEL** Listen to three students talking about how they adapt their behavior. Check (✓) the three things that they talk about.

Young people adapt their behavior to:

1. ☐ stay healthy.
2. ☐ earn money.
3. ☐ stay in touch with friends.
4. ☐ feel happy.
5. ☐ be good citizens.

**SPEAKING SKILL  Explain purpose**
Purpose is the reason for something. To explain the purpose of an action, you can use the infinitive with *to*.
  *I take shorter showers to save water.*
You can also use *help/allow* (+ person/thing) + infinitive with *to*.
  *The giraffe's long neck **helps it to reach** leaves in tall trees.*
  *It also **allows the giraffe to look out** for danger.*
You can also use *so that* + **subject** + verb.
  *The giraffe has a long neck **so that it can reach** leaves in tall trees.*

F **APPLY** Listen again and complete the sentences. Write one word in each blank.

1. I use social media _____ in touch with friends. It's the easiest way.

2. I call her or she calls me every week _____ we stay in touch.

3. For example, I spend time in nature. That _____ _____ feel happy.

4. If I don't have much time, I do a short run and I run fast. It _____ _____ get a lot of exercise in a short time.

5. I usually swim for at least half an hour, and I swim fast _____ I stay healthy.

**94** UNIT 6

Focused academic **listening** and **speaking skills** help students communicate with confidence.

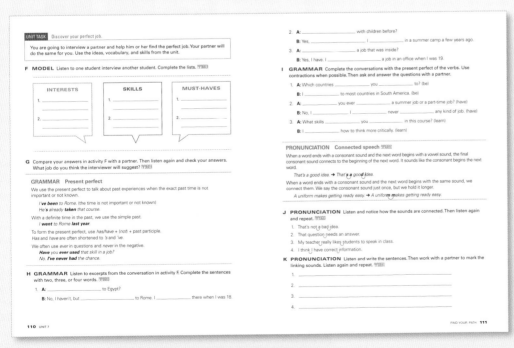

**UNIT TASK**  Discover your perfect job.

You are going to interview a partner and help him or her find the perfect job. Your partner will do the same for you. Use the ideas, vocabulary, and skills from the unit.

F **MODEL** Listen to one student interview another student. Complete the lists.

| INTERESTS | SKILLS | MUST-HAVES |
|---|---|---|
| 1. | 1. | 1. |
| 2. | 2. | 2. |

G **Compare** your answers in activity F with a partner. Then listen again and check your answers. What job do you think the interviewer will suggest?

**GRAMMAR  Present perfect**
We use the present perfect to talk about past experiences when the exact past time is not important or not known.
  *I've been to Rome.* (the time is not important or not known)
  *He's already taken that course.*
With a definite time in the past, we use the simple past.
  *I went to Rome last year.*
To form the present perfect, use *has/have* + (*not*) + past participle.
*Has* and *have* are often shortened to *'s* and *'ve*.
We often use *ever* in questions and *never* in the negative.
  ***Have** you **ever used** that skill in a job?*
  *No. **I've never had** the chance.*

H **GRAMMAR** Listen to excerpts from the conversation in activity F. Complete the sentences with two, three, or four words.

1. **A:** _____ to Egypt?
   **B:** No, I haven't, but _____ to Rome. I _____ there when I was 18.

2. **A:** _____ with children before?
   **B:** Yes, _____ I _____ in a summer camp a few years ago.

3. **A:** _____ a job that was inside?
   **B:** Yes, I have. I _____ a job in an office when I was 19.

I **GRAMMAR** Complete the conversations with the present perfect of the verbs. Use contractions when possible. Then ask and answer the questions with a partner.

1. **A:** Which countries _____ you _____ to? (be)
   **B:** I _____ to most countries in South America. (be)

2. **A:** _____ you ever _____ a summer job or a part-time job? (have)
   **B:** No, I _____. I _____ never _____ any kind of job. (have)

3. **A:** What skills _____ you _____ in this course? (learn)
   **B:** I _____ how to think more critically. (learn)

**PRONUNCIATION  Connected speech**
When a word ends with a consonant sound and the next word begins with a vowel sound, the final consonant sound connects to the beginning of the next word. It sounds like the consonant begins the next word.
  *That's a good idea. → That's **a good i**dea.*
When a word ends with a consonant sound and the next word begins with the same sound, we connect them. We say the consonant sound just once, but we hold it longer.
  *A uniform makes getting ready easy. → A unifor**m m**akes getting ready easy.*

J **PRONUNCIATION** Listen and notice how the sounds are connected. Then listen again and repeat.

1. That's not a bad idea.
2. That question needs an answer.
3. My teacher really likes students to speak in class.
4. I think I have correct information.

K **PRONUNCIATION** Listen and write the sentences. Then work with a partner to mark the linking sounds. Listen again and repeat.

1. _____
2. _____
3. _____
4. _____

**110** UNIT 7

FIND YOUR PATH **111**

**Clear models, relevant grammar, and step-by-step planning** give students the support they need to complete the final speaking task successfully.

# CONNECT TO ACHIEVEMENT

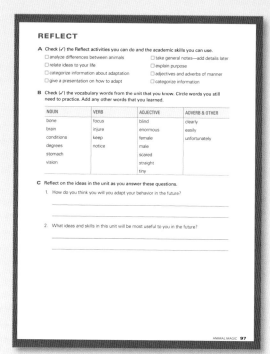

**Reflect** at the end of the unit is an opportunity for formative assessment. Students review the skills and vocabulary they have gained.

## DIGITAL RESOURCES

**TEACH** lively, engaging lessons that get students speaking. The Classroom Presentation Tool helps teachers to present the Student's Book pages, play audio and video, and increase participation by providing a central focus for the class.

## LEARN AND TRACK

with Online Practice and Student's eBook. For students, the mobile-friendly platform optimizes learning through customized re-teaching and adaptive practice. For instructors, progress-tracking is made easy through the shared gradebook.

**ASSESS** learner performance and progress with the ExamView® Assessment Suite available online.

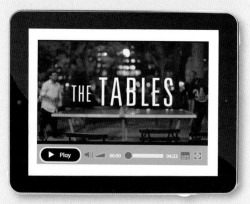

# ACKNOWLEDGMENTS

The Authors and Publisher would like to acknowledge the teachers around the world who participated in the development of *Reflect*.

A special thanks to our Advisory Board for their valuable input during the development of this series.

## ADVISORY BOARD

**Dr. Mansoor S. Almalki**, Taif University, Saudi Arabia; **John Duplice**, Sophia University, Japan; **Heba Elhadary**, Gulf University for Science and Technology, Kuwait; **Hind Elyas**, Niagara College, Saudi Arabia; **Cheryl House**, ILSC Education Group, Canada; **Xiao Luo**, BFUS International, China; **Daniel L. Paller,** Kinjo Gakuin University, Japan; **Ray Purdy**, ELS Education Services, USA; **Sarah Symes,** Cambridge Street Upper School, USA.

## GLOBAL REVIEWERS

### ASIA

**Michael Crawford**, Dokkyo University, Japan; **Ronnie Hill**, RMIT University Vietnam, Vietnam; **Aaron Nurse**, Golden Path Academics, Vietnam; **Simon Park**, Zushi Kaisei, Japan; **Aunchana Punnarungsee**, Majeo University, Thailand.

### LATIN AMERICA AND THE CARIBBEAN

**Leandro Aguiar**, inFlux, Brazil; **Sonia Albertazzi-Osorio**, Costa Rica Institute of Technology, Costa Rica; **Auricea Bacelar**, Top Seven Idiomas, Brazil; **Natalia Benavides**, Universidad de Los Andes, Colombia; **James Bonilla**, Global Language Training UK, Colombia; **Diego Bruekers Deschamp**, Inglês Express, Brazil; **Josiane da Rosa**, Hello Idiomas, Brazil; **Marcos de Campos Bueno**, It's Cool International, Brazil; **Sophia De Carvalho**, Ingles Express, Brazil; **André Luiz dos Santos**, IFG, Brazil; **Oscar Gomez-Delgado**, Universidad de los Andes, Colombia; **Ruth Elizabeth Hibas**, Inglês Express, Brazil; **Rebecca Ashley Hibas**, Inglês Express, Brazil; **Cecibel Juliao**, UDELAS University, Panama; **Rosa Awilda López Fernández**, School of Languages UNAPEC University, Dominican Republic; **Isabella Magalhães**, Fluent English Pouso Alegre, Brazil; **Gabrielle Marchetti**, Teacher's House, Brazil; **Sabine Mary**, INTEC, Dominican Republic; **Miryam Morron**, Corporación Universitaria Americana, Colombia; **Mary Ruth Popov**, Ingles Express, Ltda., Brazil; **Leticia Rodrigues Resende**, Brazil; **Margaret Simons**, English Center, Brazil.

### MIDDLE EAST

**Abubaker Alhitty**, University of Bahrain, Bahrain; **Jawaria Iqbal**, Saudi Arabia; **Rana Khan**, Algonquin College, Kuwait; **Mick King**, Community College of Qatar, Qatar; **Seema Jaisimha Terry**, German University of Technology, Oman.

### USA AND CANADA

**Thomas Becskehazy**, Arizona State University, AZ; **Robert Bushong**, University of Delaware, DE; **Ashley Fifer**, Nassau Community College, NY; **Sarah Arva Grosik**, University of Pennsylvania, PA; **Carolyn Ho**, Lone Star College-CyFair, TX; **Zachary Johnsrud**, Norquest College, Canada; **Caitlin King**, IUPUI, IN; **Andrea Murau Haraway**, Global Launch / Arizona State University, AZ; **Bobbi Plante**, Manitoba Institute of Trades and Technology, Canada; **Michael Schwartz**, St. Cloud State University, MN; **Pamela Smart-Smith**, Virginia Tech, VA; **Kelly Smith**, English Language Institute, UCSD Extension, CA; **Karen Vallejo**, University of California, CA.

# WELCOME TO THE NEIGHBORHOOD

## IN THIS UNIT

▶ Reflect on your neighborhood

▶ Give reasons for choosing your neighborhood

▶ Imagine life in Longyearbyen

▶ Present advantages and disadvantages of your neighborhood

## SKILLS

**LISTENING**
Take notes—focus on key information

**SPEAKING**
Give opinions

**GRAMMAR**
Quantifiers

**CRITICAL THINKING**
Analyze what you know and don't know

Families enjoy the evening on the central square in the town of El Carmen de Bolívar, Colombia.

## CONNECT TO THE TOPIC

1. What kind of neighborhood does this look like? Would you like to live here?

2. What makes a neighborhood a nice place to live?

# PREPARE TO LISTEN

**A VOCABULARY** Listen to the words. Complete the questions with the correct words. 🔊 1.1

| access (n) | cost (n) | grow up (v phr) | local (adj) | prefer (v) |
|---|---|---|---|---|
| busy (adj) | get around (v phr) | join (v) | nature (n) | variety (n) |

1. Is your neighborhood close to _____? I mean, is it close to forests and rivers?

2. Did you _____ and go to school there?

3. How do you _____: by car, bike, bus, or on foot?

4. Are there a lot of places to go? Is there a _____ of shops and restaurants?

5. Is the _____ of renting a house or apartment high?

6. Is it a _____ neighborhood? Are there a lot of cars and people?

7. Are the _____ people friendly?

8. Is there easy _____ to a supermarket, or do you need a car?

9. Would you _____ to live in a different neighborhood?

10. Are there any sports clubs that you can _____?

---

COMMUNICATION TIP

When we answer *yes/no* questions, we don't always answer with *Yes* or *No*. We use phrases like these:
*Yeah. Totally. / Absolutely.*
*I guess so. / Kind of.*
*Yes and no. / Not really.*
*No way! / Not at all.*

---

**B** Listen to people answer questions from activity A. Which question does each person answer? Which phrase from the Communication Tip does each one use? 🔊 1.2

1. question __10__ phrase _____

2. question _____ phrase _____

3. question _____ phrase _____

4. question _____ phrase _____

5. question _____ phrase _____

An interview in the streets
of Tokyo, Japan

**C** Listen again. Choose the reason that each person gives for their answer. 🎧 1.2

1. a. She wants more sports clubs.
   b. She doesn't want more sports clubs.
2. a. There are a lot of different apartments to rent.
   b. There are a lot of different shops.
3. a. The shops and restaurants are quite close.
   b. The shops and restaurants are quite far away.
4. a. All the local people are friendly.
   b. Some of the local people are friendly.
5. a. He thinks the cost of renting is high.
   b. He doesn't know if the cost of renting is high.

REFLECT    Reflect on your neighborhood.

You are going to listen to interviews about why people live where they do.
Think about your own neighborhood. With a partner, take turns asking and
answering the questions in activity A.

# LISTEN & SPEAK

## WHY DO YOU LIVE HERE?

Gülhane Park in Istanbul, Turkey

**A MAIN IDEAS** Listen to three street interviews. Check (✓) the correct answers. 🎧 1.3

1. Why does she live in that neighborhood?
   - ☐ It's close to her workplace.
   - ☐ It's close to a lot of tech companies.
   - ☐ She works for a tech company.

2. Why does he live in that neighborhood?
   - ☐ He grew up there.
   - ☐ His friends and family live there.
   - ☐ It's changing.

3. Why does she live in that neighborhood?
   - ☐ It's very quiet.
   - ☐ It has a big variety of shops.
   - ☐ It has a lot of places to eat out.

**B PHRASES TO KNOW** Work with a partner. Discuss the meaning of the phrases. Then practice using the phrases in sentences that are true for you.

1. That **is important to** me.
2. This city **is home to** a lot of them.
3. I just **don't care about** it now.

**C  DETAILS**  Listen to the interviews again and answer the questions.  🎧1.3
Which person (the person interviewed in 1, 2, or 3) . . .

1. _____ lives in a busy neighborhood?

2. _____ lives close to nature?

3. _____ thinks the area is changing?

4. _____ travels by bike a lot?

5. _____ wants to live in a quieter neighborhood?

6. _____ has a mother and father who lived in the neighborhood?

---

**LISTENING SKILL  Take notes—focus on key information**

When taking notes, write only key information. To recognize key information, listen for words or phrases that the speaker repeats. Listen for words the speaker says more loudly or slowly. In an interview, listen to the questions. Your notes should focus on key words but be complete enough to help you remember the important information.

> **Q:** *Why do you live here, in this neighborhood?*
> **A:** *Why do I live here? Well, let me see. The main reason is that a few of my family members and friends are here. Yeah, that's the main reason.*

NOTES:  Why live neighborhood = family + friends

---

**D  APPLY**  Look at the notes for the first interview. Which notes (1–6) are key information? Cross out the ones that are not. Then cross out words that you don't need in the notes.

**Why live in this neighborhood?**

1. She lives in the neighborhood because it's close to her workplace.

2. The job is in the city not the neighborhood.

3. She can ride to work on a bike.

4. She wanted to be close to her workplace.

5. The city is home to a lot of tech companies.

6. She wanted easy access to nature.

**E  APPLY**  Listen to interviews 2 and 3 again and take notes in your notebook. Focus on key information. Then compare your notes with a partner.  🎧1.4

## GRAMMAR  Quantifiers

Quantifiers tell how much of something we are talking about. Quantifiers sometimes depend on **the noun** (count or noncount). Count nouns are nouns that can be singular or plural. Noncount nouns are usually singular.

| COUNT NOUNS | NONCOUNT NOUNS |
|---|---|
| **A big amount** | |
| There are **a lot of / many** restaurants. | There's **a lot of** grass and greenery. |
| **An inexact amount** | |
| There are **some** shops. | There's **some** traffic during rush hour. |
| **A small amount** | |
| There are **a few** parks. | There's **a little** space here. |
| **None** | |
| There aren't **any** shopping malls. | There isn't **any** work here. |
| **Questions and answers** | |
| Are there **any** trees? | Is there **any** noise? |
| No, there aren't **any / many** trees. | No, there isn't **any / much** noise. |

Note 1: *much* and *any* are used in negatives and questions.
Note 2: *information, money, time,* and *weather* are common noncount nouns.

**F  GRAMMAR** Read the sentences. Underline the quantifiers.

1.  I'm just doing a little research.
2.  The main reason is that a few of my family members and friends are here.
3.  People have some money now.
4.  There are a lot of places to eat out.
5.  There aren't any restaurants in her neighborhood.

**G  GRAMMAR** Choose the correct quantifiers. Sometimes more than one is possible.

1.  There are **a few / a little / any** good places to eat in my neighborhood.
2.  Are there **any / much / many** theaters?
3.  People don't have **many / any / a lot of** money in this neighborhood.
4.  There are **many / a few / some** shops.
5.  There isn't **any / many / much** snow in winter.
6.  There is **a lot of / a few / any** work for people who speak English.
7.  In summer, there is **a little / a few / some** traffic in the town center.
8.  There aren't **any / many / a lot of** cafes here.
9.  Are there **any / a little / many** parks in your town?
10. **Any / A little / A lot of** people wear warm jackets in winter.

**H GRAMMAR** Complete the paragraph with quantifiers. More than one answer is possible.

I live in my neighborhood because I grew up there and because ¹_____ of my friends and family live there. I like it because it's very multicultural and there are ²_____ different people from all over the world. There are ³_____ restaurants and cafes. Also, there isn't ⁴_____ traffic, so there isn't ⁵_____ noise, which is good. There are ⁶_____ young people and families in the area, but there aren't ⁷_____ elderly people. ⁸_____ people live there because they are studying and the cost of rent is low. Other people live there because they grew up there, or because it's safe.

**I** Work with a partner. Look at the infographic and guess the three missing reasons. Listen and check your answers. What other reasons are there for choosing a neighborhood? 🎧 1.5

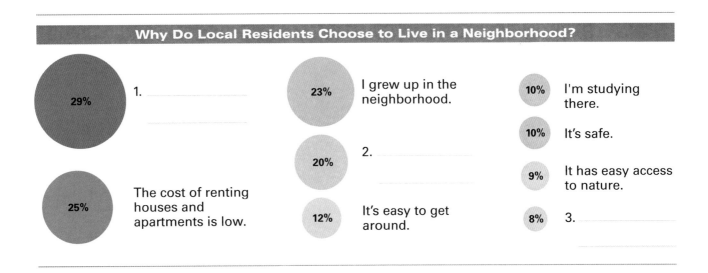

**Why Do Local Residents Choose to Live in a Neighborhood?**

29%  1. _____

25%  The cost of renting houses and apartments is low.

23%  I grew up in the neighborhood.

20%  2. _____

12%  It's easy to get around.

10%  I'm studying there.

10%  It's safe.

9%  It has easy access to nature.

8%  3. _____

**REFLECT**  Give reasons for choosing your neighborhood.

Work in small groups. Tell your group:
▸ why you live in your neighborhood
▸ why you like it
Use quantifiers and the example in activity H to help you.

# PREPARE TO WATCH

**A** **PREDICT** Work with a partner. Look at the infographic. Which facts do you think describe the Arctic region, and which ones describe Antarctica? Write *the Arctic* or *Antarctica* below each fact.

---

| The Arctic or Antarctica? |
|:---:|

1. It's land
surrounded by sea.

_____

2. It's frozen sea
surrounded by land.

_____

3. It's the coldest
place on earth.

_____

4. Penguins live there.

_____

5. Polar bears live there.

_____

6. About 4 million people
live there.

_____

7. No one lives there.

_____

8. The South Pole is there.

_____

9. The North Pole is there.

_____

---

## CRITICAL THINKING   Analyze what you know and don't know

Sometimes you hear a topic, but you don't know what it is or what it means. If this happens, don't worry. Just ask yourself some basic questions, and then ask others or research the answers online.

*What are the differences between the Arctic and Antarctica?*

**B** **APPLY** What do you want to know about the Arctic or Antarctica? Write three questions to research. Then go online to find the answers.

_____

_____

_____

_____

**C** Look at the map of Svalbard and complete the information.

Svalbard is a group of islands in the

1_____ Ocean, about

650 miles (1,050 kilometers) from the

2_____ Pole. Svalbard is part

of the country of 3_____.

Arctic Ocean
North Pole
N
Nordaustlandlet
Spitsbergen
Longyearbyen
Edgeoya
60 miles
60 km
Norway

**D** **VOCABULARY** Listen to the words. Complete the sentences with the correct form of the words. 🎧 1.6

| anyone (pron) | average (adj) | familiar (adj) | island (n) | resident (n) |
| around (prep) | destroy (v) | gun (n) | large (adj) | trip (n) |

1. Svalbard is a group of _____ in the Arctic Ocean.

2. Spitsbergen is _____. The other islands are small.

3. Over 2,000 _____ live on Svalbard.

4. On Svalbard, you need a _____ because of wild animals.

5. The _____ daytime temperature is usually below freezing.

6. _____ who visits in winter will not see the sun.

7. Because of climate change, there are more avalanches (a big wall of snow that comes down a mountain). The avalanches sometimes kill people and _____ houses.

8. The biggest town on Svalbard is Longyearbyen. There is coal in the hills _____ Long- yearbyen. In the past, there were coal mines, too.

9. Longyearbyen looks _____, like a normal town, but it is not. It is the northernmost town on Earth.

10. Tourists can visit Longyearbyen and take a _____ on a snowmobile.

---

**REFLECT**   Imagine life in Longyearbyen.

You are going to watch a video about Longyearbyen, a town on Svalbard in the Arctic. Use your imagination to complete these sentences about Longyearbyen. Then compare with a partner.

1. In Longyearbyen there is/are a lot of . . .

2. There are a few . . .

3. There isn't a . . .

4. There aren't any . . .

# LIFE IN LONGYEARBYEN

The beautiful aurora borealis, also called the northern or polar lights, above Longyearbyen

**A MAIN IDEAS** Watch the video and choose the correct answers. ▶1.1

1. a. Longyearbyen is a normal town.
   b. Longyearbyen is not a normal town.

2. a. It is closer to the North Pole than any other town.
   b. It is closer to the North Pole than most other towns.

3. a. It is easy to live here.
   b. It is difficult to live here.

4. a. There are tourists and students here.
   b. There are no tourists or students here.

**B DETAILS** Work with a partner. Complete the sentences with the numbers. Then watch again and check your answers. ▶1.1

| 0 | 2 | 10 | 50 | 100 | 800 | 2,000 |

1. There are more than _____ permanent residents.

2. There are only _____ kilometers of roads.

3. Recently an avalanche destroyed _____ houses.

4. The avalanche also killed _____ people.

**C PHRASES TO KNOW** Work with a partner. Discuss the meaning of these phrases from the video. Then correct the sentences about Longyearbyen.

1. You **are required to** carry your passport when you leave town.
2. The sun does **not** rise **at all** from February to October.
3. The economy is **shifting towards** coal mining.

**D** Work with a partner. Make sentences about Longyearbyen. Use the words below.

1. 800 miles – North Pole
2. snowmobiles – residents
3. coal – hills
4. tourists – snowmobiles and dog sleds

*The town is 800 miles from the North Pole.*

**E** Work with a partner. What are some possible advantages of living in Longyearbyen? Make a list. Then watch the video and check your ideas. ▶1.2

**F** Ask four or five people what they like and don't like about their neighborhood. Take notes on what they say. You can use these ideas for your final presentation.

The neighborhood of Barranco in Lima, Peru

| UNIT TASK | Present advantages and disadvantages of your neighborhood. |

You are going to explain the advantages and disadvantages of your neighborhood in a short talk. Use the ideas, vocabulary, and skills from this unit.

**G MODEL** Listen to someone talk about the neighborhood of Barranco in Lima, Peru. Answer the questions. 🎧 1.7

1. What is Barranco close to? _____

2. Who lives there? _____

3. What is on every wall? _____

4. What good things can you find in Barranco? _____

5. What are the local residents like? _____

6. What is not a big problem for the speaker? _____

**PRONUNCIATION  Sounds and syllables** 🎧 1.8

Each word in English has one or more syllables. Each syllable has one vowel sound and may have one or more consonant sounds. In words with more than one syllable, there is one syllable that gets the main stress. This syllable is said more loudly than the others.

| one syllable | two syllables | three syllables | four syllables |
|---|---|---|---|
| **cost** | **bu•**sy | **res•**tau•rant | va•**ri•**e•ty |

**H PRONUNCIATION** Listen and write the number of syllables in each word. Then listen again and underline the syllable that is stressed. 🎧 1.9

1. access ____2____
2. apartment _____
3. familiar _____
4. houses _____
5. local _____
6. nature _____
7. neighborhood _____
8. photography _____
9. tourist _____

**I PRONUNCIATION** Listen and complete the sentences with the words you hear. Then work with a partner. How many syllables does each word have? Take turns reading the text aloud. 🔊1.10

Barranco is on the sea so it has easy access to a variety of ¹_____. It's home to a lot of

young people and ²_____ because it's cheaper than Miraflores.

What is Barranco like? Well, it's very colorful and there is street art on every wall. There are a lot

of small ³_____ and restaurants, so you can eat many different ⁴_____. It's a

great place to take ⁵_____, and in my opinion it's a very cool place to live. There are

also a few ⁶_____ like MATE, a photography museum, and MAC, a museum of

contemporary art.

What are the advantages? Well, Barranco is easy to get around. There are some ⁷_____,

but people usually walk. There is a lot to do, and the local ⁸_____ are very friendly.

---

**SPEAKING SKILL   Give opinions**

In academic speaking, the difference between fact and opinion is important. A fact is something that is true or that you can prove. An opinion is a belief about something. When you want to give your opinion, start with a phrase that shows it's an opinion and not a fact.

*I think (that)* the best neighborhood to live in is Barranco.
*I don't think (that)* it's a big problem.
*In my opinion,* it's a very cool place to live.

This is also true when you give other people's opinions.
*In his opinion,* it is a great place to live.

---

**J APPLY** Work with a partner. Answer the questions with your opinion.

1. Do you think that traffic is a big problem in your neighborhood?
2. In your opinion, what is the best neighborhood in your town or area?
3. Do you think that there are a lot of good cafes in your area?
4. In your opinion, are the local residents friendly?

   *Q: Do you think that traffic is a big problem in your neighborhood?*
   *A: In my opinion, it's a very big problem.*

**K PLAN** Complete the chart with information about your neighborhood.

| | Notes on your neighborhood |
|---|---|
| Name of neighborhood | |
| Description: What is it like? Are there a lot of places to eat? Are there any parks? | |
| Advantages: Is it easy to get around? Are the residents nice? | |
| Disadvantages: Is it expensive/busy/crowded? | |
| Summary: Give your opinion. | |

**L PRACTICE** Use your notes from activities F and K to prepare your presentation. Practice giving your presentation to a partner.

**M UNIT TASK** Work in small groups and follow the steps:

1. Take turns presenting your neighborhood to your group.
2. As you listen to other students, take notes in the table below.
3. After all the presentations, say which neighborhood you want to move to and why.

| Name of neighborhood | Description | Advantages | Disadvantages | Speaker's opinion |
|---|---|---|---|---|
| | | | | |
| | | | | |
| | | | | |

# REFLECT

**A** Check (✓) the Reflect activities you can do and the academic skills you can use.

☐ reflect on your neighborhood

☐ give reasons for choosing your neighborhood

☐ imagine life in Longyearbyen

☐ present advantages and disadvantages of your neighborhood

☐ take notes—on key information

☐ give opinions

☐ quantifiers

☐ analyze what you know and don't know

**B** Check (✓) the vocabulary words from the unit that you know. Circle words you still need to practice. Add any other words that you learned.

| NOUN | VERB | ADJECTIVE | ADVERB & OTHER |
|---|---|---|---|
| access | destroy | average | anyone |
| cost | get around | busy | around |
| gun | grow up | familiar | |
| island | join | large | |
| nature | prefer | local | |
| resident | | | |
| trip | | | |
| variety | | | |

**C** Reflect on the ideas in the unit as you answer these questions.

1. Have your ideas about what makes a neighborhood a nice place to live changed after working through this unit?

_____

_____

2. What ideas or skills in this unit will be most useful to you in the future?

_____

_____

# OLDEST, MIDDLE, YOUNGEST

This family in Abu Dhabi, United Arab Emirates, spends every Saturday together visiting local parks, renting bikes, or riding the Ferris wheel.

## CONNECT TO THE TOPIC

1. What are the relationships between the people in the photo?

2. Do you have brothers or sisters? Would you like more siblings?

19

# PREPARE TO LISTEN

**A  ACTIVATE**  Think of words for family members and write them down. Then compare with a partner.

**B  VOCABULARY**  Listen to the words. Complete the sentences with the correct form of the words. 🎧 2.1

| careful (adj) | consider (v) | dangerous (adj) | independent (adj) | similar (adj) |
|---|---|---|---|---|
| confident (adj) | creative (adj) | difference (n) | in general (phr) | smart (adj) |

1.  My nephew, Kadir, likes doing _____ things. For example, he rides his motorcycle very fast.

2.  _____, everyone in my family gets along well. We enjoy spending time together.

3.  My grandfather, Wang Shu, is 92, but he's _____. For example, he does all his own shopping.

4.  My sister, Aiko, is _____. She doesn't make mistakes at work.

5.  My niece, Aisha, is _____. She always knows the answers in class.

6.  My nephew, Francisco, is _____. He's always sure that he is right.

7.  My aunt, Jovana, is _____. She writes short stories.

8.  My brother, Noburu, is _____ to me. We are both fun and happy.

9.  My cousin, Juliana, doesn't make decisions quickly. She _____ every option first.

10. There are a lot of _____ between my half brother, Mateo, and me. For example, he's confident but not very independent, and I'm independent but not very confident.

**C  PERSONALIZE**  Work with a partner. Use the words in activity B to talk about your family members.

*My father is creative. He plays the piano, and he paints.*

**D** Listen to four people talk about siblings. Match each country with a fact. 🎧2.2

| Country | Fact |
|---|---|
| 1. _____ Japan | a. Most children live with a sibling. About 50 percent of children have a stepsibling. |
| 2. _____ India | b. People don't use the word *cousin*. All cousins are called "brother" or "sister." |
| 3. _____ Uganda | c. There is a festival every year to celebrate brothers and sisters. |
| 4. _____ the United States | d. Children use a special name for older and younger siblings. |

**E** Compare your answers in activity D with a partner. Then listen again and check your answers. 🎧2.2

**REFLECT**    Generate ideas about sibling behavior.

You are going to listen to a talk about how siblings behave with each other. What should siblings do or not do for each other? Complete the sentences. Then compare with a partner.

Older siblings should _____

Younger siblings should _____

Siblings in Bung, Nepal

# LISTEN & SPEAK
# BIRTH ORDER THEORY

The Kanneh-Mason family performs at the British Academy Film Awards in London, England. All seven siblings in the family are musicians and often play together.

**A  PREDICT** You will listen to a lecture on birth order theory. Birth order theory tries to explain differences in sibling behavior based on whether they are the oldest, middle, or youngest. Look at the infographic with a partner. Choose words to complete the infographic.

| careful | creative | friendly | independent | popular | smart |
|---------|----------|----------|-------------|---------|-------|

## Birth Order

**FINDING** 21 of the first 23 American astronauts were oldest children.

**FINDING** A study of 2,400 Norwegian men found that oldest children had an average IQ score of 103, middle children 100, and youngest children 99.

**Oldest** children are usually confident,

1._____

and

2._____.

**Middle** children tend to be

3._____

and

4._____.

**Youngest** children are usually funny and

5._____.

**Only** children tend to be confident and

6._____.

**B  APPLY** Look at the information in activity A. Which of the two findings do you think is stronger? Explain.

**C  MAIN IDEAS** Listen to the lecture and take notes. Write the key facts and main ideas. Then check your predictions in activity A. 🎧 2.3

**D  DETAILS** Listen again. Answer the questions with two or three words. 🎧 2.3

1.  How old is birth order theory? _____

2.  What kind of activities will oldest children probably not do? _____

3.  What do middle children have compared to their siblings? _____

4.  What do youngest children get from their family when they are growing up? _____

5.  Who are only children most similar to? _____

6.  How big are the differences between siblings, according to science? _____

**E  APPLY** Which generalizations about oldest, middle, youngest, and only children do you remember from the lecture? Work with a partner and make a list. Which ones do you think are true?

**F DETAILS** Listen to excerpts from the lecture. Complete them with a word or phrase from the Communication Tip. 🎧2.4

1. . . . they usually don't do dangerous sports _____ motorcycle racing or skydiving.

2. . . . they do things that their parents don't like _____ staying out late.

3. This means that they are similar to oldest children. _____ they are often confident.

4. . . . those differences are very small. _____ oldest children tend to have a higher IQ than their siblings, but only three points higher.

**COMMUNICATION TIP**

Use these phrases to give examples:

At the beginning or in the middle of a sentence:

*For example, for instance*

Before a noun:

*like, such as*

## GRAMMAR Comparative and superlative adjectives

We use **comparative adjectives** to compare one person, thing, or group to another. We often use *than* after the comparative.

We use **superlative adjectives** to compare one person or thing to all the other people or things in a group. We usually use the word *the* before the superlative form.

Note the different forms for these adjectives.

| Adjectives | Comparative | Superlative |
|---|---|---|
| with one or two syllables ending in -y | *I've got an **older** sister.* *She's **friendlier than** me.* | *I'm **the oldest** of three daughters.* *I'm **the friendliest**.* |
| with two, three, or more syllables | *I'm **more independent than** my brother.* | *My sister is **the most independent** person in our family.* |
| irregular | good → **better** bad → **worse** | good → **the best** bad → **the worst** |

**G GRAMMAR** Underline the comparative adjectives and circle the superlative adjectives in these sentences.

1. I'm more creative than my sister, but she was always smarter than me in school.

2. I'm the most confident person in my family, but my brother is friendlier and more popular than me. He's probably the most popular person I know.

**H** Listen to four people talk about their siblings, and answer the questions. Then compare your answers with a partner. 🎧 2.5

1. Is the speaker the older, younger, or in the middle?

   Speaker 1 _____          Speaker 3 _____

   Speaker 2 _____          Speaker 4 _____

2. How many siblings does the speaker have?

   Speaker 1 _____          Speaker 3 _____

   Speaker 2 _____          Speaker 4 _____

**I** **GRAMMAR** Listen and complete the conversations with two or three words. 🎧 2.6

1. **A:** So, let's think about you and your brother. Who's more creative?

   **B:** Oh, my brother, I think. He's _____ me. He's always taking interesting photos.

2. **A:** So, think about your sister and your brother for a moment. Who's _____ _____?

   **B:** Oh, my sister, definitely. She's a doctor. She's _____ me and my brother.

3. **A:** So, think about you and your sister. Who's _____, you or your sister?

   **B:** Oh, she is, definitely.

   **A:** Really, why?

   **B:** Well, for a start she's _____ me.

**J** **GRAMMAR** Use the words to write sentences with a comparative or superlative adjective.

1. Ria / happy person / in this class. _____

2. My mother / confident / my father. _____

3. Tim / independent person / in his family. _____

4. Jenn / smart / her sister. _____

5. Who / creative person / that you know? _____

**REFLECT**  Compare yourself to siblings or friends.

Think about your siblings. If you are an only child, think about one or two friends. Which adjectives from this unit describe you? Which adjectives describe your siblings or friends?

Work with a partner. Use comparative and superlative adjectives.

*A: Do you have any brothers or sisters?*

*B: Yes, I do. I have an older brother.*

*A: Who is friendlier, you or your brother?*

# PREPARE TO WATCH

**A  VOCABULARY**  Listen to the words. Complete the sentences with the correct form of the words. 🔊 2.7

| | | | | |
|---|---|---|---|---|
| angry (adj) | argument (n) | be born (v phr) | everywhere (adv) | share (v) |
| argue (v) | attention (n) | chore (n) | get along (v phr) | wonder (v) |

1.  If I have a(n) _____ with a friend, I feel bad and I don't like it. That's why I'm always nice to my friends.

2.  I _____ my things with my friends. If my friend wants to use my car or my bike, for example, that's fine.

3.  When I was younger, I wanted my parents' _____. I wanted them to talk to me and ask me questions.

4.  As a child, I had small jobs to do in the house. For example, I put the dishes in the dishwasher after every meal. I always did my _____ as fast as possible.

5.  My best friend and I go _____ together. We are almost never apart.

6.  I never _____ with my sister. We're very similar and we're always friendly to each other.

7.  I _____ what it's like to have a lot of brothers and sisters. I don't know, but I think it's probably fun.

8.  I sometimes get _____ with my brother. He asks me a lot of questions about my private life, and I don't like that.

9.  I _____ in June. It's my favorite month because we celebrate my birthday.

10. Some of my friends don't _____ with their brothers or sisters. They don't like each other, and they fight a lot.

**B**  Work with a partner. Say which sentences in activity A are true for you. Change the other sentences to make them true for you.

*If I have an argument with a friend, I don't really mind. It's normal to have arguments with friends.*

**C** What do you know about sibling competition or rivalry? Work with a partner to complete the quiz.

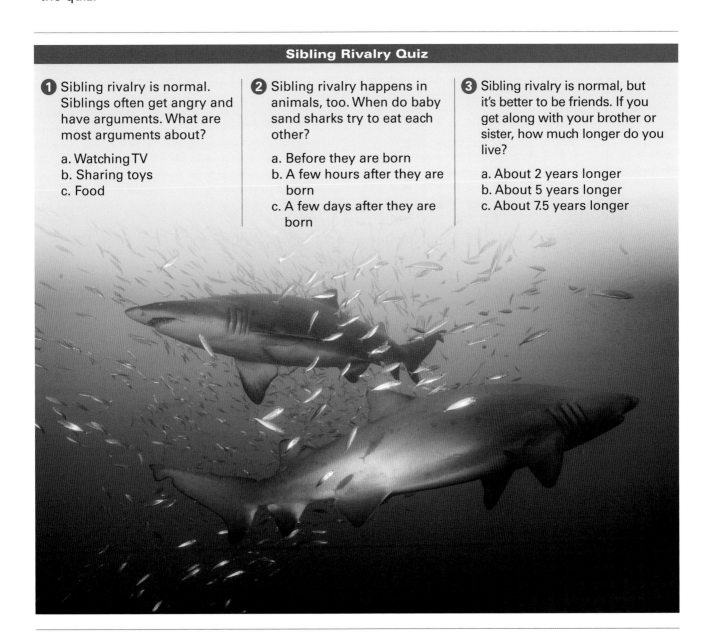

**Sibling Rivalry Quiz**

**1** Sibling rivalry is normal. Siblings often get angry and have arguments. What are most arguments about?

a. Watching TV
b. Sharing toys
c. Food

**2** Sibling rivalry happens in animals, too. When do baby sand sharks try to eat each other?

a. Before they are born
b. A few hours after they are born
c. A few days after they are born

**3** Sibling rivalry is normal, but it's better to be friends. If you get along with your brother or sister, how much longer do you live?

a. About 2 years longer
b. About 5 years longer
c. About 7.5 years longer

**D** Listen and check your answers to the quiz in activity C. Then work with a partner. Discuss which fact is most surprising to you and why. 🔊 2.8

**REFLECT**    Relate ideas to your experiences.

You are going to watch a video about a boy's relationship with his brother. Think about your own childhood. Work with a partner and discuss these questions.

1. Who did you argue with the most when you were a child?

2. What did you argue about?

3. How did you solve your arguments?

# MY BIG BROTHER

**A PREDICT** Look at the image. How do you think the boy feels about his big brother?

**B MAIN IDEAS** Watch the video. Write T for *True* or F for *False*. ▶ 2.1

1. _____ The boy has a special brother.

2. _____ It's always fun to have a brother like that.

3. _____ Overall, he's happy that he has a special brother.

**C PHRASES TO KNOW** Complete the sentences with a phrase from the video. Then discuss with a partner. Which sentences are true for you?

| get lost in | hand-me-downs | my style |
|---|---|---|

1. When I was growing up, I wore _____ from my older siblings and cousins.

2. I didn't like formal clothes. I usually wore sports clothes. They were more _____ .

3. I often _____ my imagination and forget to do my chores.

**D DETAILS** Watch the video again. Complete each sentence with one word. ▶ 2.1

This is my big brother.

When he was [1]_____ the doctor said it was a miracle.

My mom said, "You'd better believe it"!

I wonder what it would be like growing up with a [2]_____ brother.

The hand-me-downs might be more of my [3]_____ .

Games would be a little easier, and for once I could be [4]_____ than him at something.

Mom says I should be happy I [5]_____ have a brother to play with, but sometimes, he's too much brother.

He does get the [6]_____ done fast.

And he gives me rides everywhere.

Sometimes, I feel like I get lost in his shadow.

But life with a normal brother would [7]_____ be so much smaller.

**E DETAILS** Discuss the questions with a partner.

1. What does the boy think about the hand-me-downs from his big brother?
2. Who is always better at games, the boy or his brother?
3. What are two advantages of having this big brother?

**F** Think about famous siblings or siblings in stories. Do the siblings get along with each other? Tell your partner about the siblings.

This boy's big brother is especially big.

You are going to give a short presentation about two siblings that you know. You will describe both siblings and compare them. Use the ideas, vocabulary, and skills from the unit.

**G MODEL** Listen to two people talk about siblings. Complete the chart. 🔊2.9

| Names | Rosamie and Jasmine | Stefan and Francisco |
|---|---|---|
| Similarities | | |
| Differences | | |
| Problems | | |

**H** Work with a partner and compare your answers in activity G. Then listen again and check. 🔊2.9

**PRONUNCIATION** The schwa /ə/ 🔊2.10

The schwa /ə/ is an unstressed vowel sound. It can be the sound of any vowel in an unstressed syllable or word. You don't open your mouth much to say the schwa sound. It is the most common sound in English.

The underlined sound or sounds in these words is a schwa.

| /ə/ | /ə/ | | /ə/ | /ə/ |
|---|---|---|---|---|
| a-tten-tion | pro-blem | | a-gain | |

**I PRONUNCIATION** Listen to the words and underline the syllables with the schwa. Circle the syllable with the stress. Then listen again and repeat the words. 🔊2.11

1. ad-vice
2. e-ven
3. care-ful
4. un-der-stand
5. con-fi-dent
6. a-long

**J PRONUNCIATION** Listen to this excerpt from the model and write the missing words. The missing words all have a schwa sound. 🔊2.12

Hello. I'm Stefan and I'm going to talk ¹_____ my stepbrother, Francisco.

Francisco is 19 years old, so he's one year younger ²_____ me. We get

³_____ very well. Francisco grew up in ⁴_____ country, but now

he lives here. Like me, he's ⁵_____, friendly, ⁶_____ he loves sports.

## SPEAKING SKILL   Ask for and give advice

To ask for advice, use these questions.

*What's your advice?*
*What do you think I should do?*
*Do you have any advice?*

Use these phrases to give advice.

*I think he should say sorry.*
*I don't think you should be angry with him.*
*Perhaps/Maybe they should talk to each other more.*
*Why don't you give her more attention?*

**K  APPLY**  Use the words and phrases to write sentences, asking for and giving advice.

1.  think / he / be more independent.

    I think he should be more independent.
    _____.

2.  perhaps / you / listen to her more.

    _____.

3.  not think / she / take her clothes without asking.

    _____.

4.  Why / you / help him?

    _____.

5.  What / think / I / say?

    _____.

6.  maybe / they / stop fighting / talk more.

    _____.

**L**  Work with a partner. What is your advice to these people?

**Rosamie:** My sister comes into my bedroom and takes my clothes without asking. What do you think I should do?

**Stefan:** My brother wants to be a professional soccer player, but he's not good enough. He's smart, but he doesn't study because he's always playing soccer. What's your advice?

**M PLAN** Think about two siblings that you know (one of the siblings can be you). Complete the chart with information about the two siblings. You will use these notes to give your presentation.

|  | You/Sibling 1 | Sibling 2 |
|---|---|---|
| Details: What are their names? How do you know them? |  |  |
| Similarities: In what ways are they similar? |  |  |
| Differences: In what ways are they different? |  |  |
| Fights and Problems: What do they argue about? Are there any problems between them? |  |  |

**N PRACTICE** Work in groups of three or four. Practice your presentations. Use the chart in activity M to help you.

**O UNIT TASK** Give your presentation to the class. As you listen to other students, take notes in the chart.

| Details of siblings | Similarities between them | Differences between them | Fights and problems |
|---|---|---|---|
|  |  |  |  |

# REFLECT

**A** Check (✓) the Reflect activities you can do and the academic skills you can use.

- ☐ generate ideas about sibling behavior
- ☐ compare yourself to siblings or friends
- ☐ relate ideas to your experiences
- ☐ give a presentation about siblings

- ☐ recognize generalizations
- ☐ ask for and give advice
- ☐ comparative and superlative adjectives
- ☐ evaluate information

**B** Check (✓) the vocabulary words from the unit that you know. Circle words you still need to practice. Add any other words that you learned.

| NOUN | VERB | ADJECTIVE | ADVERB & OTHER |
|------|------|-----------|----------------|
| argument | argue | angry | everywhere |
| attention | be born | careful | in general |
| chore | consider | confident | |
| difference | get along | creative | |
| | share | dangerous | |
| | wonder | independent | |
| | | similar | |
| | | smart | |

**C** Reflect on the ideas in the unit as you answer these questions.

1. What do you think are the advantages and disadvantages of having siblings?

_____

_____

2. What ideas or skills in this unit will be most useful to you in the future?

_____

_____

# 3 | I'M A BIG FAN

Friends play music together in Morocco's Tinghir Province.

- Discuss your experiences with music
- Make a playlist
- Evaluate a music survey
- Present the results of a survey

## SKILLS

**LISTENING**
Take notes using symbols

**SPEAKING**
Make and respond to suggestions

**GRAMMAR**
Question forms

**CRITICAL THINKING**
Recognize reliable research

## CONNECT TO THE TOPIC

1. How do the people in the photo feel? Why?
2. How important is music in your life?

35

# PREPARE TO WATCH

**A ACTIVATE** How many types of music do you know? Make a list and then compare with a partner.

*traditional, pop*

**B** Listen to two people talk about music. Choose the correct answers. 🎧 3.1

1. Clio **likes / doesn't like** traditional Greek music.

2. Glen **likes / doesn't like** classical music.

3. Clio **likes / doesn't like** classical music.

4. Glen **likes / doesn't like** jazz.

**C** Listen again and complete the sentences. 🎧 3.1

**Glen:** What sort of music do you like, Clio?

**Clio:** Well, I ¹_____ traditional Greek music.

**Glen:** Traditional Greek music?

**Clio:** Yeah, my mother's from Greece. What about you, Glen?

**Glen:** I'm a big ²_____ of classical music. I listen to it every day.

**Clio:** Really? I ³_____ it. Sorry, but I find it so boring!

**Glen:** You don't know what you're missing! Do you like jazz?

**Clio:** It's OK. I don't ⁴_____ it. What about you?

**Glen:** It's my least favorite kind of music. I can't ⁵_____ it.

**D** Listen and match the music excerpts to the words. Compare your answers with a partner. 🎧 3.2

| classical | country | hip-hop |
|-----------|---------|---------|
| jazz | pop | rock |

1. _____        4. _____

2. _____        5. _____

3. _____        6. _____

**E** Read the Communication Tip. Then work with a partner. Which types of music do you like? Which don't you like?

> **COMMUNICATION TIP**
>
> When we say that we like or don't like something, we often use words such as:
>
> **love, be a fan of**
>
> *I love traditional Japanese music.*
>
> *I'm a big fan of classical music.*
>
> **can't stand, hate**
>
> *I can't stand jazz.*
>
> *I hate pop music.*
>
> **it's OK, don't mind**
>
> *I don't mind hip-hop.*

**F VOCABULARY** Listen to the words in **bold**. Match the sentences with similar meaning. 🎧 3.3

1. _____ I'm **alone**.

2. _____ I'm **annoyed**.

3. _____ I feel **connected** to you.

4. _____ I **disagree**.

5. _____ I play an **instrument**.

6. _____ It's **loud**.

7. _____ They are happy **memories**.

8. _____ It's **old-fashioned**.

9. _____ It **reminds** me of you.

10. _____ It's a **stadium**.

a. I remember you when I see or hear it.

b. It's not modern in style.

c. They are things that we like to remember.

d. It's a big place to watch sports or music.

e. I'm unhappy.

f. I feel close to you because we share so much.

h. It's not quiet.

g. I have a different opinion.

i. I make music with something, for example, a guitar.

j. There aren't any people with me.

**G** Choose the correct form of a word in **bold** from activity F to complete each question.

1. Have you ever been to a big concert in a _____?

2. Can you play a musical _____, like the guitar or the piano?

3. Which song has happy _____ for you?

4. Do any of your neighbors play _____ music? Is it a problem for you?

5. What is your favorite song? What does it _____ you of?

6. Who is your favorite singer? Do your friends agree or _____ with you?

7. What music do you listen to when you are _____ at home?

8. Do you get _____ when you hear the same song over and over?

9. Do you have any CDs, or are they _____ technology from the past?

10. Who is your favorite singer? Do you feel _____ to other fans of that singer?

**REFLECT** Discuss your experiences with music.

You are going to watch a video about music. Think about your own experiences. Ask and answer the questions in activity G with a partner.

# WHY DO WE DISAGREE ABOUT MUSIC?

**A PREDICT** In this video, you will learn why we have different opinions about music. What three reasons do you think you will hear?

We disagree about music because . . .

a. we hear different sounds from the same music.

b. we are different ages.

c. we have different memories.

d. we like disagreeing.

e. music gives us an identity (an idea of who we are).

People dance at a silent disco at the Open'er Festival in Gdynia, Poland.

**B MAIN IDEAS** Watch the video. Complete the summary with one word in each sentence. ▶ 3.1

Music is universal. We play it at the most ¹_____ times in our lives, but we also disagree

about music a lot. One reason is age: The music we like when we are a ²_____ is

our favorite music for life. Another reason is that music brings back different ³_____ for

different people. A final reason is that music is important for our identity. It helps us feel

⁴_____ to some people and different from others.

**C PHRASES TO KNOW** Complete the sentences with phrases from the video. Then tell
a partner which sentences you agree with.

| brings back | is not as good as | makes me happy |
|---|---|---|

1. Music from recent years _____ music from before.

2. Dance music always _____.

3. Listening to music often _____ memories.

**D DETAILS** Watch again and complete each sentence with two words. ▶ 3.1

1. Every society has music and _____ _____.

2. We listen to music when we _____ _____, and when loved ones die.

3. We listen to music when we are alone, and when we are in _____ _____.

4. Some people think that music came _____ _____.

5. On average, people first hear their favorite song when they are _____
   _____ old.

6. For most people, music from _____ _____ is not as good as older music.

7. Music brings back memories from our teenage years and our _____
   _____.

8. Many people like a song because it reminds them of a _____ _____.

**E** Work with a partner. Who do you talk to about music? Do the people you talk to agree or
disagree with you about music? Explain.

*I talk to my friend Esther about music. We usually agree, but sometimes we disagree because . . .*

## PRONUNCIATION   Word stress 🎧3.4

To say a word correctly, you need to know which syllable is stressed. A stressed syllable is louder, longer, and clearer than the other syllables in the word.

▸ Most two-syllable nouns and adjectives have stress on the first syllable.

**con**cert     **neigh**bors     **nor**mal

▸ Most two-syllable verbs have stress on the second syllable.

ar**rive**     in**vite**     be**gin**

**F PRONUNCIATION** Listen and notice the stress. Then listen again and repeat. 🎧3.5

1. **sing**er
2. con**nect**
3. **bor**ing
4. en**joy**
5. **re**cent
6. **an**gry
7. pre**fer**
8. **rea**son
9. com**pare**

**G PRONUNCIATION** Work with a partner. Underline the stressed syllable in the bold words. Then listen and check your answers. Repeat the sentences. 🎧3.6

1. Every **country** and every **culture** has **music**.
2. Some **people believe** that music came before **language**.
3. Many people like a song if it **reminds** them of their **teenage** years.

**H** Listen to two friends discuss music for an end-of-semester karaoke party. Which two songs do they choose? 🎧3.7

| Singer/band | Song title |
|---|---|
| Shakira and Rihanna | 1. |
| Girls' Generation | 2. |

Friends sing karaoke in Tokyo, Japan.

## SPEAKING SKILL  Make and respond to suggestions

| Make Suggestions | Respond - Agree | Respond - Disagree |
|---|---|---|
| Let's choose some songs to sing. | Good idea. | I'd prefer not to. |
| Should we sing some pop music? | Sure. | I don't know. |
| What about that song by Beyoncé? | OK. | I'm not sure. |
| Why don't we sing a Shakira song? | Why not? | I don't think that's a good idea. |
| How about singing *Memories*? | | |

**I**  Listen again. Complete each sentence with one or two words. 🎧 3.8

**A:** ¹_____ that song by Shakira and Rihanna? What's it called?

**B:** Oh, *Can't Remember to Forget You*?

**A:** That's right. *Can't Remember to Forget You.*

**B:** Yes, great song.

**A:** And ²_____ singing Macarena?

**B:** Um, I'm not sure. It's a great song, but it's a little old now.

**A:** Yeah, I guess you're right.

**B:** Some K-pop songs are in English. ³_____ we sing one of those?

**A:** Good idea. I love K-pop.

**B:** ⁴_____ *The Boys* by Girls' Generation? That's mostly in English.

**A:** What was that again?

**B:** *The Boys* by Girls' Generation.

**A:** OK. ⁵_____ add it to the list.

**B:** ⁶_____ invite some friends now?

**A:** Good idea.

REFLECT   Make a playlist.

Work with a partner and make a playlist for a karaoke party. Decide on songs that you would both enjoy singing. Use the language in the Speaking Skill box.

*A: Let's start with a song by Shakira.*

*B: Good idea.*

# PREPARE TO LISTEN

**A VOCABULARY** Listen to the words and phrases. Complete the questions. 🎧 3.9

| | | | | |
|---|---|---|---|---|
| convenient (adj) | digital (adj) | last (adj) | spend (v) | surprising (adj) |
| crazy about (adj phr) | global (adj) | percent (n) | streaming (adj) | well-known (adj) |

1. When was the _____ time you listened to music? What did you listen to?

2. How much time do you _____ listening to music every day?

3. How important is music to you? Are you _____ it, or do you find it unimportant?

4. Do you listen to a music _____ service? If so, which one?

5. Is all your music _____, or do you still own CDs and records?

6. Who do you think is the most _____ singer in your country?

7. What _____ of people in your country use their smartphone to listen to music?

8. What is easier and more _____: downloading music or streaming music? Why?

9. What do you think is the most exciting _____ trend or current style in music?

10. What was the most _____ hit song of last year? Why is it strange that it was a hit?

**B** Work with a partner and compare your answers in activity A. Then ask each other the questions.

**C** Read the information about the average music listener. Which facts are true for you? Discuss with a partner.

According to the Music Listening Survey by IFPI[1], the average music listener . . .

▸ listens to about 2½ hours of music a day.
▸ listens to a digital streaming service for about 4 hours a week.
▸ spends 5.4 hours a week listening to the radio.

[1] IFPI stands for International Federation of the Phonographic Industry. It is an organization that represents the recorded music industry worldwide.

## CRITICAL THINKING   Recognize reliable research

To be reliable, a research survey must ask questions to a lot of different people. When you see research results from a survey, ask yourself these questions:

*How many people took part in the survey?*
*What were the ages of the participants?*
*Where were the participants from?*

**D APPLY** Choose the most likely numbers to complete the sentences about the survey that IFPI did. Then listen and check your answers. 🎧 **3.10**

**Music Survey by IFPI**

[1] **34 / 34,000 / 34 million** people took part in the survey.

The people were between [2] **6 and 16 / 16 and 24 / 16 and 64**.

The people came from [3] **2 / 21 / 210** different countries.

**REFLECT**   Evaluate a music survey.

You are going to listen to the results of IFPI's survey. Work with a partner and discuss the questions.

1. What do you think of the IFPI research survey?
2. How could it be made more reliable?

# LISTEN & SPEAK

## A GLOBAL
# MUSIC LISTENING SURVEY

**A PREDICT** Look at the infographics and predict the missing information from the IFPI survey. Compare your predictions with a partner.

### 1. Spent money on music in the last month

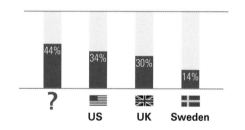

44%  34%  30%  14%

?  US  UK  Sweden

### 2. Crazy about music

75%  62%  62%  59%  54%

?  US  Mexico  Canada  Global

### 3. Devices* used to listen to music

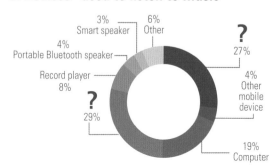

3%
Smart speaker

6%
Other

4%
Portable Bluetooth speaker

?

27%

Record player
8%

4%
Other
mobile
device

?

29%

19%
Computer

### 4. Favorite type of music

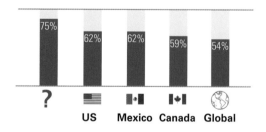

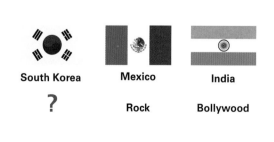

South Korea  Mexico  India

?  Rock  Bollywood

*device = a thing or machine, such as a cell phone or tablet, that helps you do something

**B MAIN IDEAS** Listen to the survey results. Check your predictions in activity A. Then complete the sentences. [3.11]

1. People in _____ spend more money on music than any other nation.

2. More than _____ of the world say that they are crazy about music.

3. We spend more time listening to music on a _____ than on a smartphone.

4. The most popular kind of music in South Korea is _____.

**C PHRASES TO KNOW** Match the numbers in the box to the words in bold.

| 1/3 | 1/2 | 3/4 |
|-----|-----|-----|

1. _____ So, more than **half** of the world is crazy about music.

2. _____ Almost **one-third**, or 29%, of music listening time is on a radio.

3. _____ **Three-quarters** of South Africans are crazy about music.

---

**LISTENING SKILL   Take notes using symbols**

When taking notes, use symbols to help you write more quickly. These are common symbols.

| % → percent | hrs → hours | = → equals, is, are |
|-------------|-------------|---------------------|
| & → and | k → thousand | w/ → with |
| e.g. → for example | v. → very | + → more than |

*The survey is from an organization called IFPI, and more than 34,000 people took part.*

survey = from IFPI & 34k+ people took part

---

**D APPLY** Listen again and take notes using symbols and numbers. [3.11]

**E DETAILS** Use your notes to correct these sentences. Check your answers with a partner.

1. 44% of all people spent money on music in the last month.

   _____

2. 54% of all people said that music was not important to them.

   _____

3. Around the world about half of music listening time is on a radio.

   _____

4. The most popular type of music around the world is Bollywood.

   _____

Present the results of a survey.

You are going to survey or ask people about music. You will present the results to your classmates. Use the ideas, vocabulary, and skills from the unit.

---

## GRAMMAR Question forms

### Yes/No questions

▸ If the main verb is *be*, put it before the subject.

**Are** *you a music lover?*

▸ For the simple present, use the auxiliaries *do/does* before the subject. For the simple past, use *did*.

**Do** *you like music?*       **Did** *she buy new headphones?*

### Wh- questions

▸ Put the question word (+ noun) before the auxiliary verb.

**What** *do you listen to?*       **Which concert** *did you go to?*

▸ *How* is often followed by *many, much, often, far,* or *long.*

**How much music** *do they buy?*

---

▸ When the question word is the subject of the sentence, do not use an auxiliary verb.

**What** *happened next?*       **Who** *likes your band?*

---

**F GRAMMAR** Write *yes/no* questions using the words given.

1. **A:** I don't go to stadium concerts.

   **B:** (you / go / smaller concerts?) _Do you go to smaller concerts?_

2. **A:** I don't listen to pop music while studying.

   **B:** (you / listen / classical music?) _____

3. **A:** I didn't listen to her new album.

   **B:** (you / listen / first album?) _____

4. **A:** Two of my friends are in a band.

   **B:** (be / their band / popular?) _____

5. **A:** My brother has a musical ear.

   **B:** (he / play / a musical / instrument?) _____

**G GRAMMAR** Write *Wh-* questions for the missing information.

1. My favorite singer is __?__.

   *Who is your favorite singer?*

2. The type of music that I like best is __?__.

   _____

3. When I was younger, I listened to __?__.

   _____

4. My favorite song to sing along to is __?__.

   _____

5. The radio station I listen to the most is __?__.

   _____

6. My least favorite type of music is __?__.

   _____

**H MODEL** Listen to a student presenting the results of his survey. Complete each question with two words. 🔊3.12

Question 1: Where do you _____ _____ to music?

Question 2: What _____ do you usually _____ to listen to music?

Question 3: How often do you _____ _____ when you listen to music?

**I** Match the beginning and ending of each question.

1. __d__ Where do you usually listen          a. study?

2. _____ What music do you          b. you want to meet?

3. _____ Does listening to music help you          c. type of music?

4. _____ What was the last          d. to music?

5. _____ Which singer do          e. listen to when you are sad?

6. _____ What is your least favorite          f. concert that you went to or watched on TV?

**J PLAN** Choose a topic. Write three questions connected to that topic.

| Live music | Music habits | Music and emotions |
|---|---|---|
| Music stars | Music genres | Advantages and disadvantages of music |

_____

_____

_____

_____

**K** Before the next class, ask your questions from activity J to at least 5 people. Take notes on their answers and complete the chart. Use percentages and numbers to describe the results.

| | |
|---|---|
| Information about the participants (How many? How old? Where from?) | |
| Question 1 & results | |
| Question 2 & results | |
| Question 3 & results | |
| What did you find surprising about the results? | |

**L PRACTICE** Work in groups of three or four. Practice giving the results of your survey.

**M UNIT TASK** Present the results of your survey to another group. As you listen to your classmates, take notes in the chart. What do you think were the most interesting results?

| The participants | Question 1 & results | Question 2 & results | Question 3 & results | What was surprising? |
|---|---|---|---|---|
| | | | | |
| | | | | |

# REFLECT

**A** Check (✓) the Reflect activities you can do and the academic skills you can use.

- ☐ discuss your experiences with music
- ☐ make a playlist
- ☐ evaluate a music survey
- ☐ present the results of a survey
- ☐ take notes using symbols
- ☐ make and respond to suggestions
- ☐ question forms
- ☐ recognize reliable research

**B** Check (✓) the vocabulary words from the unit that you know. Circle words you still need to practice. Add any other words that you learned.

| NOUN | VERB | ADJECTIVE | ADVERB & OTHER |
|------|------|-----------|----------------|
| instrument | disagree | alone | |
| memory | remind | annoyed | |
| percent | spend | connected | |
| stadium | | convenient | |
| | | crazy about | |
| | | digital | |
| | | global | |
| | | last | |
| | | loud | |
| | | old-fashioned | |
| | | streaming | |
| | | surprising | |
| | | well-known | |

**C** Reflect on the ideas in the unit as you answer these questions.

1. What is the most interesting thing you learned about music in this unit?

   _____

   _____

2. What ideas or skills in this unit will be most useful to you in the future?

   _____

   _____

# THE BEAUTY
# OF SCIENCE

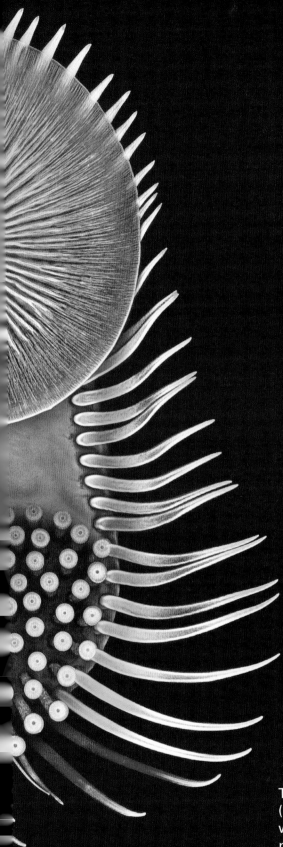

## IN THIS UNIT

▸ Understand steps in research

▸ Discuss a personal experiment

▸ Describe a home science experiment

▸ Present the results of a science experiment

## SKILLS

**LISTENING**
Understand cause

**SPEAKING**
Explain results

**GRAMMAR**
Simple past

**CRITICAL THINKING**
Consider more than one cause

The front foot of an insect (a beetle), is colored with different dyes and photographed through a microscope.

## CONNECT TO THE TOPIC

1. Describe what you see in the photo.

2. Would you like to work in science?

# PREPARE TO LISTEN

**A VOCABULARY** Listen to the words. Match the words with the definitions. 🔊 4.1

| | | | | |
|---|---|---|---|---|
| disease (n) | fall (v) | heavy (adj) | light (n) | prove (v) |
| experiment (n) | gravity (n) | hit (v) | medicine (n) | scientist (n) |

1. _____ move or drop to the ground

2. _____ a person who studies or works in science

3. _____ opposite of light in weight

4. _____ something that you take when you are ill or sick

5. _____ to touch someone or something quickly and with force

6. _____ an illness

7. _____ something that allows us to see things

8. _____ the force that pulls things toward each other and to the ground

9. _____ to show that something is true

10. _____ a test to learn something new

**B VOCABULARY** Work with a partner. Read the sentences. Which ones do you think are true, and which ones are false? Write T for *True* or F for *False*.

**Science Fact or Science Fiction?**

1. _____ If a penny falls from a very tall building and hits someone on the ground, it can kill them.

2. _____ Gravity makes heavy things fall faster than light things.

3. _____ It takes 8 minutes for light from the sun to reach Earth.

4. _____ Malaria has killed more people than any other disease in history.

5. _____ Before Albert Einstein became a brilliant scientist, he was a very bad student at school.

**C** Listen to five conversations and check your answers in activity B. 🔊 4.2

A classroom science experiment

**D** Listen again. Complete the sentences with one or two words. Then check your answers with your partner. 🎧 4.2

1. The penny might hurt you, but it wouldn't _____ you.

2. Gravity _____ heavier things fall faster than lighter things.

3. The sun is 93 _____ from Earth.

4. Malaria has killed more people than any other _____ in history.

5. Einstein was always a good student, but he didn't like the way of _____.

**E** Discuss the questions with a partner.

1. Which science facts surprised you? Explain.

2. What problems need more scientific research at the moment? Explain.

REFLECT    Understand steps in research.

You are going to learn about three science experiments. Work with a partner. These are the stages of scientific research. Put them in the correct order (1–4). Explain your choices.

| | | |
|---|---|---|
| **Experiment** ☐ | | **Question/Problem** ☐ |
| Do an experiment to test your idea. Record the data. | | Think of a question or a problem that needs an answer. |
| **Conclusion** ☐ | | **Idea** ☐ |
| Does the experiment prove that your idea is right? | | Think of an idea that might answer the question or solve the problem. |

# THREE SCIENCE EXPERIMENTS THAT CHANGED THE WORLD

*Camera obscura* means "dark chamber." When light enters a dark space through a small hole, the light makes an upside-down image of what is outside the space. This room is a camera obscura. The trees from outside in Central Park, NY, USA, are upside down and shown on the walls.

**A** Listen to the lecture and take notes. Focus on the main ideas and use symbols. 🎧 4.3

**B** **MAIN IDEAS** Use your notes and choose the correct answer.

1. What did Alhazen's experiment show?

   a. We see when light enters our eyes.

   b. We see because we have light in our eyes.

   c. We need lamps to see.

2. What did Galileo's experiment show?

   a. Heavy things fall faster than light things.

   b. Heavy things fall at the same speed as light things.

   c. Heavy things fall slower than light things.

3. What did Tu Youyou's experiment show?

a. Artemisinin comes from the plant *Artemisia annua*.

b. Artemisinin can help people with malaria.

c. Artemisinin is not safe for people with malaria.

**C DETAILS** Listen again. Write T for *True* or F for *False*. Then correct the false statements. 🎧 4.3

**Alhazen**

1. _____ Alhazen was born 1,000 years ago in Egypt.

2. _____ There were two lamps outside the room and a small hole in the wall.

3. _____ The two lamps made one spot of light on the wall.

**Galileo**

4. _____ Galileo dropped two similar balls from the Leaning Tower of Pisa.

5. _____ The two balls hit the ground at the same time.

6. _____ On the moon, the hammer hit the ground before the feather.

**Tu Youyou**

7. _____ Tu and her team wanted to find a new medicine for malaria.

8. _____ Tu made a medicine called artemisinin from a plant.

9. _____ Nobody dies from malaria anymore.

**D PHRASES TO KNOW** Work with a partner. Discuss the meaning of these phrases from the listening. Then use the phrases to say something about Alhazen and Tu Youyou.

1. Galileo **was interested in** gravity.

2. He **carried out** an experiment with two balls.

---

**LISTENING SKILL   Understand cause**

To explain the cause of an event, we often use *because* followed by a clause (subject + verb).

> They believed this **because it seemed natural**.

We can also use *because of* and *due to* followed by a noun, noun phrase, or pronoun.

> They believed we can see **because of a light in our eyes**.

> **Due to her interest in plants,** Tu Youyou began studying traditional plant medicines.

---

**E** Listen to a description of another experiment. What was the disease, and what was the "medicine"? 🎧 4.4

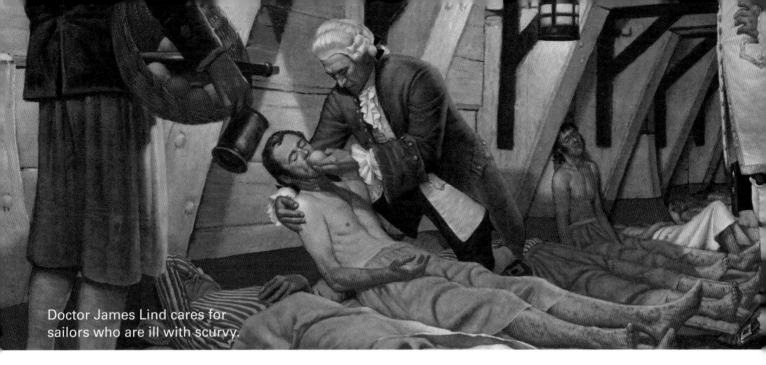

Doctor James Lind cares for sailors who are ill with scurvy.

**F APPLY** Listen again. Then complete each sentence with one or two words. 🎧 4.4

1. Many of the sailors died _____ the disease.

2. We now know that sailors got scurvy _____ they didn't have enough vitamin C.

3. The two sailors got better _____ the vitamin C in the oranges and limes.

4. British sailors took limes on long trips and _____ this, they got the name "limeys."

**G NOTICE THE GRAMMAR** Underline the regular simple past verb forms. Circle the irregular past verb forms.

In 1747, a Scottish doctor, James Lind, wanted to find a cure for scurvy. He believed that poor diet was the cause of the disease. He decided to carry out an experiment. He found some sailors with scurvy. He gave oranges and limes to two of the sailors. Those two sailors got better quickly. The others didn't get better.

---

### GRAMMAR  Simple past

We use the simple past to talk about completed actions and events in the past.
   *He **wanted** to find a cure for scurvy. He **gave** oranges to sailors.*

Regular verbs end in *-d* or *-ed* in the simple past.
   *believe* → *believe**d**   want* → *want**ed***

Many common verbs are irregular.
   *be* → ***was/were**   do* → ***did**   go* → ***went**   think* → ***thought**   have* → ***had***

We use *didn't* + the base form of the verb in negatives.
   *The others **didn't get** better.*

We use (Question word +) Did + subject + base form in questions.
   ***Did he find** a cure? Why **did they get** better?*

---

**H GRAMMAR** Complete the sentences with the simple past form of the verbs.

**Problem:** This ¹_____ (happen) to me a few months ago. I ²_____ (notice) that something was wrong. When I ³_____ (go) to bed, I couldn't sleep because I ⁴_____ (not feel) tired.

**Idea:** I ⁵_____ (decide) to try an experiment with coffee.

**Experiment:** Before the experiment, I ⁶_____ (drink) four cups of coffee every day. For the experiment, I ⁷_____ (stop) drinking coffee for two weeks. It ⁸_____ (not be) easy!

**Conclusion:** When I stopped drinking coffee, I ⁹_____ (not have) sleeping problems. After two weeks, I ¹⁰_____ (start) drinking coffee again, and the sleeping problems ¹¹_____ (come) back. My experiment ¹²_____ (prove) that coffee was the cause of the problem.

---

**PRONUNCIATION** *-ed* endings 🎧4.5

▸ Remember to pronounce an additional syllable only when *-ed* is added after a verb ending in a *-t* or *-d*.

    list-en (2 syllables) ⟶ list-ened (2 syllables; no additional syllable)
    re-port (2 syllables) ⟶ re-port-ed (3 syllables; additional syllable)

▸ Remember that the *-ed* can sound like /t/, /d/, or /ɪd/.

---

**I  PRONUNCIATION** Write the number of syllables of each past tense verb. Circle the pronunciation of *-ed*. Then listen and repeat each word. 🎧4.6

| | | | | |
|---|---|---|---|---|
| 1. watched | _____ | /t/ | /d/ | /ɪd/ |
| 2. noticed | _____ | /t/ | /d/ | /ɪd/ |
| 3. wanted | _____ | /t/ | /d/ | /ɪd/ |
| 4. happened | _____ | /t/ | /d/ | /ɪd/ |
| 5. talked | _____ | /t/ | /d/ | /ɪd/ |
| 6. needed | _____ | /t/ | /d/ | /ɪd/ |

**J** Listen to the experiment from activity H. Then work with a partner. Take turns reading the experiment aloud to each other. 🎧4.7

**REFLECT**  Discuss a personal experiment.

Think of a time when you carried out a personal experiment to solve a problem or answer a question (for example, feeling tired, having headaches, not meeting enough new people). Tell your partner about your experiment. Use activity H to help you.

# PREPARE TO WATCH

**A VOCABULARY** Listen to the words. Match the words with the definitions. 🎧 4.8

| explode (v) | light (v) | pour (v) | push (v) | rise (v) |
| go out (v phr) | mix (v) | pull (v) | react (v) | toward (prep) |

1. _____ to stop burning

2. _____ in the direction of someone or something

3. _____ to move up

4. _____ to move closer

5. _____ to change; to respond to something

6. _____ to break up into pieces, usually with noise

7. _____ to move away

8. _____ to move a liquid from one place to another

9. _____ to put two or more things together

10. _____ to make something start burning

A girl makes giant bubbles.

**B** Work with a partner and take the quiz. Then listen and check your answers. How many did you get correct? 🎧 4.9

---

Did you pay attention when you studied science at school? Take our quiz and find out.

1. Hydrogen (H) is the most common element in the universe. Helium (He) is the second most common. What happens when you mix them?
   a. They **explode**.
   b. They don't **react**.

2. It is a gas, like air, but you can **pour** it like water. If you pour it on a candle, the candle **goes out**. Which one is it?
   a. Carbon dioxide ($CO_2$)
   b. Hydrogen (H)

3. Which one will explode when you **light** it with a match?
   a. A balloon filled with hydrogen (H)
   b. A balloon filled with helium (He)

4. Every magnet has two poles, a north and a south. What happens when you place the north pole of one magnet next to the south pole of a different magnet?
   a. They **push** apart.
   b. They **pull** together.

5. What happens when you **mix** oil and water together?
   a. The oil **rises** to the top.
   b. The water rises to the top.

---

**C** Discuss the questions with a partner.

1. Are you good at science?

2. Imagine you are a scientist. What would you prefer to study? Why?

   a. the oceans      b. space      c. diseases

When explaining step-by-step processes, use *First,… Next, / Then / And then… Finally, …* to order the steps.

> *First, you take a bottle of diet soda. Then you take some mint candies…*

**REFLECT**   Describe a home science experiment.

You are going to watch some home science experiments. Work with a partner. Look at the list of home science experiments. Check (✓) the ones you have done. Add any others. Tell your partner what happened.

☐ collect and identify leaves
☐ make a parachute for an egg
☐ put a tennis ball on a football and drop them
☐ blow across the open top of a bottle

☐ make giant bubbles
☐ collect insects
☐ put an egg in a cup of vinegar
☐ put different things in the freezer

# SCIENCE YOU CAN DO AT HOME

**A PREDICT** Look at the names of the experiments you will watch. What do you think will happen in each experiment? Tell a partner.

1. Milk, food coloring, and soap
2. A balloon and water
3. A candle, water, and a glass
4. Mint candies in diet soda

**B MAIN IDEAS** Watch the video and take notes. Check your predictions in activity A. Then use your notes and match the number of the experiment to the result. ▶ 4.1

a. _____ It explodes out of the bottle.

b. _____ It looks like a firework.

c. _____ The water rises up.

d. _____ It makes a kind of electricity.

Fritz Grobe and Stephen Voltz perform the "mint candies in diet soda experiment" in New York, NY, USA. They used 646 mint candies and 122 bottles of diet soda to create these fountains of soda.

**C DETAILS** Watch again. There are two mistakes in the steps for each experiment. Correct the mistakes. ▶ 4.1

| Experiment 1 |
|---|
| 1. Pour a little milk into a cup. |
| 2. Drop some food coloring in the center of the milk. |
| 3. Drop a little water into the food coloring. |

| Experiment 3 |
|---|
| 1. Take a glass with vinegar. |
| 2. Put a candle on top. |
| 3. Light the candle. |
| 4. Put a bottle over the candle. |

| Experiment 2 |
|---|
| 1. Take a balloon and fill it with water. |
| 2. Rub the balloon on your sweater. |
| 3. Turn on the tap. |
| 4. Move the balloon away from the water. |

| Experiment 4 |
|---|
| 1. Take a bottle of diet soda and drink it. |
| 2. Take some mint candies. |
| 3. Drop the candies into the bottle. |
| 4. Step forward. |

**D** Work with a partner and answer the questions.

1. Which experiment did you like the most?

2. Have you ever done any of these experiments? If so, what happened?

3. Which experiment do you think was the easiest to do?

You are going to watch or do a science experiment and then present the results. Choose one of the options for the experiment. Use the ideas, vocabulary, and skills from the unit.

1. Do an experiment from this unit at home.

2. Watch a science experiment online.

3. Find a new experiment and do it at home.

**E  MODEL**  Listen to a student report back on an experiment. Complete the chart. Then work with a partner and check your answers. 🔊4.10

| | |
|---|---|
| Question/Problem | |
| Idea | |
| Experiment: What was the experiment and what were the steps to test the idea? | |
| Conclusion: What happened? Why did it happen? | |

**SPEAKING SKILL   Explain results**

To explain the result of an event or an action, we often use *and so* or *and as a result*. They join the cause to the result.

> *The boat wasn't very strong, **and so** it also sank after a few seconds.*
>
> *It sank as soon as he got in, **and as a result**, he fell in the water.*

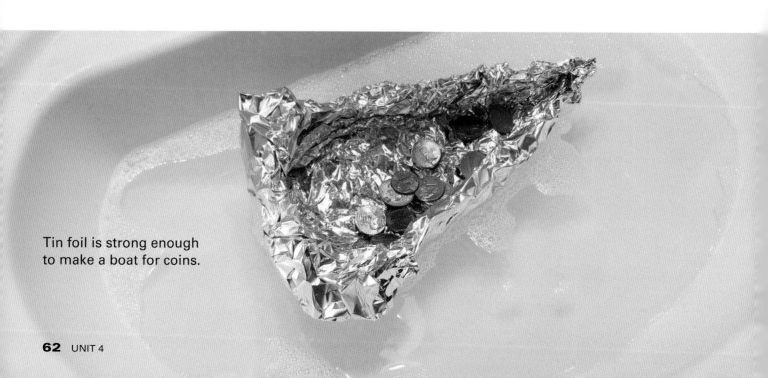

Tin foil is strong enough to make a boat for coins.

**F APPLY** Match an event to a result and join the two clauses with *and so* or *and as a result*.

**Events:**

1. I poured carbon dioxide onto a candle, ___*and as a result, it went out.*___

2. I lit a match next to a balloon filled with hydrogen, _____

3. I dropped a watermelon and an orange at the same time, _____

4. I put the north pole of one magnet next to the north pole of another magnet, _____

_____

5. The sailors with scurvy ate oranges and limes, _____

**Results:**

    a. It exploded.

    b. They got better.

    c. It went out.

    d. They hit the ground together.

    e. They pushed apart.

---

**CRITICAL THINKING  Consider more than one cause**

In a science experiment, it's easy to come to the wrong conclusion. People often think that something is a cause when really it's not. It's important to consider other possible explanations for the cause of an event. For example, you make a cake, and it doesn't taste good. You think you did not follow the directions. But maybe one of the ingredients was bad.

---

**G** Read this conclusion. Work with a partner to answer the questions.

    Amy went into town on a hot day and noticed that a lot of people wore sunglasses. She also noticed that a lot of those people ate ice cream. A few days later, Amy went into town on a cold day. She noticed that not many people wore sunglasses and not many people ate ice cream. She concluded that wearing sunglasses makes people eat more ice cream.

1. What did Amy notice on a hot day? On a cold day?

_____

2. What was her conclusion?

_____

3. Why was her conclusion wrong?

_____

**H PLAN** Complete the chart with notes about the experiment that you carried out or watched. You will use these notes to report back to the class.

| Question/Problem | |
|---|---|
| Idea | |
| Experiment | |
| Conclusion | |

**I PRACTICE** Work in groups of three or four. Use your notes in activity H to practice reporting your experiment.

**J UNIT TASK** Present the results of your experiment to the class. As you listen to other students, take notes in the chart. Which experiment did you find the most interesting?

| Question/Problem | | | |
|---|---|---|---|
| Idea | | | |
| Experiment | | | |
| Conclusion | | | |

# REFLECT

**A** Check (✓) the Reflect activities you can do and the academic skills you can use.

☐ understand steps in research      ☐ understand cause

☐ discuss a personal experiment      ☐ explain results

☐ describe a home science experiment      ☐ simple past

☐ present the results of a science experiment      ☐ consider more than one cause

**B** Check (✓) the vocabulary words from the unit that you know. Circle words you still need to practice. Add any other words that you learned.

| NOUN | VERB | ADJECTIVE | ADVERB & OTHER |
|------|------|-----------|----------------|
| disease | explode | heavy | toward |
| experiment | fall | | |
| gravity | go out | | |
| light | hit | | |
| medicine | light | | |
| scientist | mix | | |
| | pour | | |
| | prove | | |
| | pull | | |
| | push | | |
| | react | | |
| | rise | | |

**C** Reflect on the ideas in the unit as you answer these questions.

1. Which science experiment from this unit did you find the most interesting?

_____

_____

2. What ideas or skills in this unit will be most useful to you in the future?

_____

_____

# UNIT
# 5 | WHY WE BUY

Tourists shop for local crafts and souvenirs at the famous Khan el-Khalili market in Cairo, Egypt.

## IN THIS UNIT

▶ Consider your spending habits

▶ Discuss how social media impacts your spending

▶ Evaluate your money skills

▶ Present a video giving tips

## SKILLS

**LISTENING**
Predict lecture content

**SPEAKING**
Give tips

**GRAMMAR**
Present continuous

**CRITICAL THINKING**
Analyze and evaluate advice

## CONNECT TO THE TOPIC

1. What do you think of the market in the photo? Where do you shop?

2. What is the best way to save more and spend less?

# PREPARE TO LISTEN

**A ACTIVATE** How many words related to money and buying things do you know? Work with a partner and write them down.

_____

_____

**B** Work with a partner and guess the correct answer for each statement. Then listen and check your answers. 🎧 5.1

The average American:

- eats out twice or three times [1]**a week / a month / a year**.

- goes to the movies five times [2]**per week / per month / per year**.

- orders takeout once [3]**a week / a month / a year**.

- goes shopping for clothes once every [4]**two weeks / two months / two years**.

- shops online several times [5]**a week / a month / a year**.

**C** Discuss with a partner: How often do you do the activities in activity B?

_I eat out about once every two weeks._

Moviegoers enjoy popcorn.

**D VOCABULARY** Listen to the words. Complete the sentences with the correct form of the words. ◖◗ 5.2

| another (det) | bill (n) | can afford (v phr) | credit card (n) | make (v) |
|---|---|---|---|---|
| bank account (n) | borrow (v) | collect (v) | fee (n) | post (v) |

1. I already have two pairs of sneakers, but I still want _____ pair.

2. I _____ to eat out only once a month, but no more because it's so expensive.

3. Some of my friends _____ things like shoes or Star Wars toys. I don't because it's an expensive hobby.

4. When I eat out, I often _____ a photo of my food to social media.

5. Every month, the money that goes out of my _____ is more than the money that goes in. It's a problem.

6. I never _____ money from friends. It can cause problems, especially if I can't pay it back quickly.

7. I think people should spend less money than they _____. If they spend more, they will have problems.

8. I never carry cash. I use a(n) _____ to pay for everything.

9. Sometimes, my monthly cell phone _____ is really high.

10. With some credit cards, you pay a yearly _____. That's why I don't have any credit cards.

**REFLECT** Consider your spending habits.

You are going to hear a lecture about spending trends. Think about your habits. Tell your partner which statements in activity D are true for you. Change the others to make them true for you.

*A: I already have five pairs of sneakers, but I still want another pair.*

*B: Really? Why is that?*

*A: I just love sneakers. I can never have too many!*

# SPENDING MORE, **SAVING LESS**

---

**LISTENING SKILL   Predict lecture content**

When you predict the content of a lecture, you can use information that you already know, such as the topic and the title of the lecture, to guess the information that will come. Predicting is useful before and during a lecture.

BEFORE THE LECTURE

Read the title of the lecture and think about the topic. Use this information to predict what you will hear.

DURING THE LECTURE

Listen actively. Check your predictions and make new ones.

---

**A  APPLY** You are going to listen to an economics lecture. It is titled "Modern Spending Habits." Predict what you will hear.

Compared to the past, most people are

a.  spending more money.        b. saving more money.

**B**  Listen to part 1 of the lecture and check your prediction in activity A. 🎧 5.3

**C**  Listen again and answer the questions. 🎧 5.3

　　1.　How much of their money did Canadians save 40 years ago? _____

　　2.　How much of their money do Canadians save now? _____

**D MAIN IDEAS** Part 2 of the lecture is two interviews with shoppers. Listen and answer the questions. 🎧 5.4

1. What is the woman buying, and why?

   _____

2. What is the man buying, and why?

   _____

**E DETAILS** Listen again and complete the sentences with two or three words. 🎧 5.4

Interview 1

1. She buys a new purse _____.

2. She is going to pay with her credit card because her _____ is empty.

Interview 2

3. All his friends buy _____.

4. He doesn't save any money because he doesn't _____ enough.

**F** In the final part of the lecture, we hear why people spend more money than they save. With a partner, discuss why this may be true. Then listen and check your ideas. What is the main reason people spend more money now? 🎧 5.5

**G** Discuss the questions in a small group.

1. How often do you and your friends post photos of things you buy?

2. How often do you and your friends post photos of restaurant meals?

3. Do you think that you spend more because of social media?

A woman shops for shoes in Hefei, China.

## PRONUNCIATION    Rhythm and stress 🔊5.6

**Rhythm** is the pattern of stressed and unstressed syllables in a sentence. The rhythm of English sentences comes from the **stress** on certain words. Look at the rhythm of this sentence.

   It **gets** a **lot** of at**ten**tion.

▸ The **main stress** is usually on the **content words**, such as verbs, nouns, and adjectives. If a content word has more than two syllables, only stress the syllable with the main stress.

▸ The **unstressed** words are usually **structure words**, such as pronouns, auxiliary verbs, and articles. They are pronounced less loud and less clear.

**H  PRONUNCIATION** Listen and underline the stressed words. 🔊5.7

   1.  When we buy a new purse, we post a photo.

   2.  When we buy a new pair of sneakers, we post a photo.

   3.  We want to tell everybody, and we want our friends to see.

**I  PRONUNCIATION** Underline the syllables that you think will be stressed. Then listen, check, and repeat. 🔊5.8

   1.  Why are you buying another one?

   2.  We're spending more money and saving less money.

   3.  I don't make a lot of money.

   4.  Do you also save money for a rainy day?

   5.  We think it's normal, and so we want to do it.

**J  NOTICE THE GRAMMAR** Choose the correct verbs. Discuss your answers with a partner. Can you make a rule for the two forms? Then work with a partner to practice the conversation.

**A:** So, I see ¹ **you look / you're looking** at a new purse. Why ² **do you want / are you wanting** it?

**B:** I'm crazy about purses! ³ **I have / I'm having** more than 10.

**A:** So why ⁴ **do you buy / are you buying** another one?

**B:** Why not?  All my friends ⁵ **buy / are buying** a lot of purses.

**A:** How often ⁶ **do you buy / are you buying** a new purse?

**B:** I ⁷ **buy / am buying** a new one every six months.

## GRAMMAR  Present continuous

We use the present continuous to talk about:

1. Actions that are happening now, at the moment of speaking.

   *You**'re buying** new sneakers. Why **are** you **buying** them?*

2. Actions that are happening around this time.

   *We**'re saving** less and **spending** more these days.*

We often use phrases such as *now*, *at the moment*, and *these days* with the present continuous.

| **Affirmative:** subj + *be* + verb + *-ing*<br>***You're buying** a new purse.* | **Negative:** subj + *be* + *not* + verb + *-ing*<br>***We're not/We aren't saving** a lot of money.* |
| --- | --- |
| **Yes/No questions:** *be* + subj + verb + *-ing*<br>***Are you saving** money at the moment?* | **Wh- questions:** question word + *be* + subj + verb + *-ing*<br>***Why are you buying** another one?* |

Verbs of emotion, thought, and sense are not normally used in the continuous. These are called *nonaction verbs*. Examples include: *like, love, believe, want, see.* Use the simple present instead.

~~*Are you liking it?*~~ **Do you like it?**

**K GRAMMAR** Use the simple present or present continuous of the verbs to complete the sentences.

1. She _____ a new purse because she really wants it. She

   _____ a new purse every two months. (buy)

2. The lecturer _____ economics at a university. Today, she

   _____ a class about spending and saving. (teach)

3. He _____ when he's not well. Today, he has the flu so he

   _____. (not work)

4. I _____ my mother because it's her birthday. I usually

   _____ her at least twice a week. (text)

5. They're not here at the moment. I think they _____. They

   _____ every Friday evening. (eat out)

REFLECT   Discuss how social media impacts your spending.

**Discuss the questions with a partner. Explain your answers.**

1. When you see a product posted on social media, do you want to buy it?

2. When your friends post their shopping on social media, do you want to shop, too? Do you shop even if you can't afford it?

# PREPARE TO WATCH

**A** Answer two questions about money. Then listen and check your answers. 🎧 5.9

1. Your local cafe has a special: Pay one-third less for your coffee, or get one-third more coffee for the normal price. Which choice is better?

   a. pay one-third less

   b. get one-third more

   c. They are the same.

2. You buy a notepad and a pen for $1.10. The notepad costs $1.00 more than the pen. How much does the pen cost?

   a. 5 cents

   b. 10 cents

   c. 15 cents

**B VOCABULARY** Listen to the words. Match the words with the definitions. 🎧 5.10

| discount (n) | instead of (prep) | likely (adj) | rent (n) | transfer (v) |
| extra (adj) | lend (v) | on sale (phr) | skip (v) | waste (v) |

1. _____     to use too much or use badly

2. _____     the money you pay to live in a house or apartment when it's not yours

3. _____     more than usual

4. _____     to move from one place to another

5. _____     to not do something that you usually do

6. _____     in place of someone or something

7. _____     an amount of money less than the normal price

8. _____     describes something that will probably happen

9. _____     to give something to someone for a short time, not forever

10. _____     at a lower price for a short period of time

**C PERSONALIZE** Choose the responses to make the sentences true for you. Then share your answers with a partner.

1. I often borrow / don't often borrow something from a friend **instead of** buying it.
2. I often **lend** / don't often **lend** books and clothes to friends.
3. If I want to buy something, I wait / don't wait until it is **on sale**.
4. I sometimes / never **waste** money on clothes.
5. I think / don't think it's important to **transfer** money to a savings account every month.
6. I think / don't think that **rents** are too high in this town.
7. I am **likely** / not **likely** to eat at expensive restaurants.
8. I sometimes / never ask for a **discount** when I buy something at a market.
9. I often / hardly ever **skip** my daily exercise.
10. I think / don't think it's helpful to have **extra** money put away in case of an emergency.

**D** Look at the infographic. Tell a partner which information is true for you. Do you think the information is true for most people your age?

## Do You Have Good Money Skills?

**According to recent surveys,…**

| 80% of adults | 76% of adults | 61% of teens | 42% of teens |
|---|---|---|---|
| didn't learn money skills in school. | don't have basic money skills. | don't know how much money they have to spend every month. | don't ask, "Can I afford it?" before they buy something. |

REFLECT    Evaluate your money skills.

You are going to watch a video about ways to save money. Work with a partner and complete the tasks below.

1. Choose the sentence that best describes you. Explain your answer.
   ▸ I have good money skills.
   ▸ I have average money skills.
   ▸ I have poor money skills.

2. Explain what money skills you need to learn.

   *I need to learn to save some money every month.*

# EIGHT MONEY-SAVING TIPS

Check out your local library to save money instead of buying books.

**A PREDICT** Look at the tips. Work with a partner and guess the missing word(s) in each.

1. Turn off the _____ an hour before you go to bed.

2. Don't go shopping. Spend some time in _____.

3. Don't always buy books. Go to the _____ instead.

4. Open a(n) _____ at the bank.

5. Have a(n) _____ before you go shopping.

6. Cut your own _____.

7. Don't buy your daily _____. Make it at home.

8. Learn to say "I can't _____ it."

**B MAIN IDEAS** Watch the video. Check your predictions in activity A and write the correct words. ▷5.1

**C PHRASES TO KNOW** Work with a partner. Discuss the meaning of these phrases from the video. Then take turns answering the questions.

1. What can **keep** you **from** making good choices at the supermarket?
2. Have you **checked out** your local library recently?
3. Where do you often see **tons of** people?

**D DETAILS** Watch the video again. Match a tip in activity A with a reason or method below. ▷5.1

a. _____ You save between two and three pounds every day.

b. _____ It's cheaper than buying books.

c. _____ You don't need the heat when you are in bed.

d. _____ Even if the salesperson offers you a discount.

e. _____ You won't spend money on food you don't need.

f. _____ It's also a great way to get extra exercise.

g. _____ You can learn how to do it online.

h. _____ You can transfer some money each month, so you don't spend it.

**CRITICAL THINKING   Analyze and evaluate advice**

When you hear a tip or someone suggesting you do something, ask yourself if it is good advice. Use logic and experience to decide if the tip will work.

For example, you hear: "Make your own clothes! It's a great way to save money."

Stop and evaluate the advice. Is making your own clothes possible for you? It's only a good tip if you have the right skills and enough time.

**E  APPLY** Look again at the tips in activity A. Evaluate each tip and choose:

▸ two tips that you think will work and will save you money.
▸ two tips that you think won't work and won't save you money.

Explain your choices to a partner.

*I think that borrowing books from a library will work because . . .*

**UNIT TASK**   Present a video giving tips.

You are going to make a "top tips" video. Use the ideas, vocabulary, and skills from the unit.

**F  MODEL** Listen to a speaker giving tips. Complete the chart. Then compare answers with a partner. 🔊5.11

| Topic (problem) | |
|---|---|
| Tip 1 | |
| Tip 2 | |
| Tip 3 | |

## SPEAKING SKILL   Give tips

There are a variety of ways to give tips. The most common is the imperative form.

> ***Don't buy*** *coffee.* ***Make*** *it instead.*

You can use *never* and *always* with the imperative.

> ***Never buy*** *books.* ***Always borrow*** *them instead.*

The imperative can sound very direct. These sentences are less direct.

> ▸ ***Try to have*** *a snack before you go.*
> ▸ ***If it's*** *winter,* ***turn off*** *the heat.*
> ▸ ***Maybe you can open*** *a savings account.*

People respond more positively to a tip if you explain the benefits.

> ***It's a great way to*** *keep from spending money.*
> ***It will help you to*** *spend less.*
> ***This means that*** *you can save a ton of money.*

**G APPLY** Listen and complete the tips with three or four words. 🎧5.12

1. Just walk up those stairs. It's _____ get in shape.

2. These exercises _____ get stronger without joining a gym.

3. Learn to cook fresh food. _____ you'll eat less sugar and less salt.

**H APPLY** Discuss with a partner. Complete the sentences with your own tips and benefits.

1. _____. It will help save you a ton of money.

2. If you hate exercising alone, _____.

3. Make a to-do list. It's a great way to _____.

4. Spend a few minutes alone every day. This means that _____.

5. _____. It's a great way to learn English.

**I PLAN** Work in small groups. Choose one of these topics for your video (or choose your own). Then complete the chart.

▸ How to take a good photo
▸ How to get a lot of online followers
▸ How to be successful at school or at work

| Topic | |
|---|---|
| Tip 1 | Benefit |
| Tip 2 | Benefit |
| Tip 3 | Benefit |

**J PRACTICE** Practice giving your tips and benefits in your group. Make sure that everyone presents at least one tip and benefit.

**K UNIT TASK** Use a smartphone to make a video of your group giving its "top tips." You can edit it to include music and special effects. Present your video to the class. As you watch the other videos, take notes in the chart. Which videos have tips you can use?

| | Topic | Tips | Benefits |
|---|---|---|---|
| Video 1 | | | |
| Video 2 | | | |
| Video 3 | | | |

# REFLECT

**A** Check (✓) the Reflect activities you can do and the academic skills you can use.

☐ consider your spending habits

☐ discuss how social media impacts your spending

☐ evaluate your money skills

☐ present a video giving tips

☐ predict lecture content

☐ give tips

☐ present continuous

☐ analyze and evaluate advice

**B** Check (✓) the vocabulary words from the unit that you know. Circle words you still need to practice. Add any other words that you learned.

| NOUN | VERB | ADJECTIVE | ADVERB & OTHER |
|------|------|-----------|----------------|
| bank account | borrow | extra | another |
| bill | can afford | likely | instead of |
| credit card | collect | | on sale |
| discount | lend | | |
| fee | make | | |
| rent | post | | |
| | skip | | |
| | transfer | | |
| | waste | | |

**C** Reflect on the ideas in the unit as you answer these questions.

1. What did you learn about your spending habits while studying this unit?

_____

_____

2. What ideas and skills in this unit will be most useful to you in the future?

_____

_____

# 6 | ANIMAL MAGIC

A leaf-tailed gecko in Andasibe-Mantadia National Park, Madagascar

## IN THIS UNIT

▸ Analyze differences between animals

▸ Relate ideas to your life

▸ Categorize information about adaptation

▸ Give a presentation on how to adapt

## SKILLS

**LISTENING**
Take general notes—add details later

**SPEAKING**
Explain purpose

**GRAMMAR**
Adjectives and adverbs of manner

**CRITICAL THINKING**
Categorize information

## CONNECT TO THE TOPIC

1. Can you find the animal in this photo?

2. Which animals are good at living in cities? What have they learned to do?

# PREPARE TO WATCH

**A ACTIVATE** How many parts of an animal's body can you name? Make a list. Then compare your list with a partner.

_____

_____

**B VOCABULARY** Listen to the words. Then choose a word to complete the questions. 🎧 6.1

| | | | | |
|---|---|---|---|---|
| blind (adj) | degrees (n) | focus (v) | scared (adj) | unfortunately (adv) |
| clearly (adv) | easily (adv) | notice (v) | tiny (adj) | vision (n) |

1. When you read on your phone, do you need glasses to see _____?

2. Is your long-distance _____ good without glasses?

3. Do you always _____ if a friend has a new haircut?

4. How many _____ of vision do you think a human has (a full circle is 360)?

5. Can you _____ remember people if you have seen their face before, or is it difficult for you?

6. When they are tired, some people find it difficult to _____ on the words in a book or magazine. The words are hard to see. Is this true for you?

7. Some people are afraid of the dark. Do you sometimes get _____ when you can't see in the dark?

8. Do you know anyone who is completely _____ and can't see at all?

9. _____, some people have red and itchy eyes in summer. Do you sometimes experience this?

10. With a microscope you can see _____ things, for example, bacteria, very clearly and easily. Have you ever used a microscope?

**C PERSONALIZE** Work with a partner. Check your answers to activity B. Then take turns asking and answering the questions.

**D** Read the statements. Then use the phrases in the Communication Tip to tell a partner which ones you think are facts and which ones are myths (things that many people believe, but that are not true).

HUMAN VISION: FACTS AND MYTHS

1. Humans have better vision and see more clearly than all other animals.
2. Your eyes are the same size now as they were when you were born.
3. Only men can be colorblind.
4. It's dangerous to look straight at the sun.
5. Reading in a dark room will hurt your eyes.
6. Eating carrots will help you see more easily and clearly at night.

**E** Listen and check your answers to activity D. 🔊6.2

REFLECT    Analyze differences between animals.

You are going to watch a video about how animals see. Look at the photos and discuss the questions with a partner.

1. What is the main difference between the wolf's eyes and the sheep's eyes?
2. What are some differences in how the two animals live?
3. What might be a reason for the difference in their eyes?

# THE WORLD THROUGH ANIMAL EYES

Damselflies have compound eyes with thousands of tiny lenses.

**A PREDICT** Work with a partner. Look at the title of the video, the photo, and the caption. In what ways do you think animals, such as horses and birds, and insects, such as bees and flies, see differently from humans?

**B** Watch the video. In your notebook, take notes on the key ideas. Then check your predictions in activity A. ▶ 6.1

**C MAIN IDEAS** Read the sentences and write T for *True* or F for *False*.

1. _____ Cows see the world in the same way as humans.

2. _____ Horses and cows both have a blind spot.

3. _____ Humans have better vision than birds.

4. _____ Insect eyes are very different from human eyes.

5. _____ Fish all have the same kind of eyes and vision.

**D PHRASES TO KNOW** Complete the sentences with a phrase from the video. Compare your answers with a partner.

| in general | the advantage of | find it difficult |
|---|---|---|

1. Cows _____ to focus because their eyes are far apart.

2. _____ compound eyes is that they allow insects to see all around.

3. _____, deep-sea fish are good at seeing in low light.

**E** Work with a partner. Take turns asking and answering the questions.

1. In general, do you prefer to learn about people or animals?
2. What is the advantage of having four legs?
3. Do you find it difficult to take notes while you watch a video?

**F DETAILS** Watch the video again. Check (✓) the sentences that are true. Then compare your answers with a partner. ▶ 6.1

1. ☐ Cows see the world in red and orange.
2. ☐ Cows have 120 degrees of vision.
3. ☐ You shouldn't stand behind a horse.
4. ☐ Horses have the best vision of all animals.
5. ☐ Birds can see ultraviolet light.
6. ☐ Eagles can see much farther than humans.
7. ☐ Most insects can see all around.
8. ☐ Deep-sea fish can't see in low light.

**G NOTICE THE GRAMMAR** Look at the words in bold. Which word describes a thing and which describes an action?

> *Most birds have very **good** vision. They see the world **clearly**.*

---

## GRAMMAR Adjectives and adverbs of manner

### Adjectives

▸ describe nouns (things and people) and usually come before a noun.
> *Insects can see **bright** colors.*

▸ can come after the verb *be*.
> *The insect is **small**.*

▸ do not have a plural form.
> *Their eyes are **tiny**.*

### Adverbs of manner

▸ describe verbs (actions). They tell us how something happens.
> *A horse might kick you **hard**.*

▸ usually come after a verb or the object of the verb.
> *Birds fly **fast**.*
> *Birds see the world **clearly**.*

▸ are often formed with adjective + *-ly*.
> *happy – **happily**   slow – **slowly**   quick – **quickly**

Notice these irregular adverbs:
> good – **well**   *She plays soccer **well**.*
> hard – **hard**   *We all work **hard**.*
> fast – **fast**   *He speaks **fast**.*

---

**H GRAMMAR** Listen and complete the sentences with one word. Then compare your answers with a partner. Is each word an adjective or an adverb? 🎧 6.3

Many people think bats are ¹_____. In fact, most bats have

²_____ vision and they can see ³_____. But because bats fly

⁴_____ and at night, they also need to use their ears. Some bats have

⁵_____ ears, and they can hear very ⁶_____.

It is a common myth that bats are blind.

**I GRAMMAR** Complete the sentences. Use the correct adjective and adverb form of the words.

1. Did you know that elephants are _____ swimmers? Humans have to learn to swim, but elephants don't. They swim _____. (natural)

2. Lyrebirds are really _____ actors. They can copy the sounds of other birds very _____. (good)

3. Emperor penguins work _____ to look after their babies. They walk 30 miles to the sea to get fish for them. That's _____ work for an animal with short legs! (hard)

4. Squirrels are _____ learners. They watch each other, and they learn new ways to get food. They learn _____. (quick)

5. Different animals can be good friends and live together _____. For example, some birds live with crocodiles and often go inside the crocodile's mouth. Both animals are _____ with this situation. (happy)

6. Sloths are very _____ animals. They sleep for 15 hours a day and, when awake, they move very _____ through the trees. On average, they travel just 123 feet (37.5 meters) per day. (slow)

7. Cats often bring mice home for their owners because they think that humans are _____ hunters and need help. This is true, of course. Compared to cats, we hunt mice very _____. (bad)

8. For polar bears, swimming is very _____. They can _____ swim for several hours without stopping, and scientists have recorded one polar bear swimming for nine days without stopping. (easy)

---

REFLECT    Relate ideas to your life.

Think about the animals from the video, bats, and other animals you know. Work with a partner. Take turns asking and answering the questions.

1. Which animal's vision do you want?

2. Which animal's vision do you not want?

# PREPARE TO LISTEN

**A  ACTIVATE** How many different kinds of animals do you know? Make a list. Then compare your list with a partner.

_____

_____

**B  VOCABULARY** Listen to the words. Match the words to the definitions. Use a dictionary if necessary. 6.4

| | | | | |
|---|---|---|---|---|
| bone (n) | conditions (n) | female (adj) | keep (v) | stomach (n) |
| brain (n) | enormous (adj) | injure (v) | male (adj) | straight (adj) |

1. _____ very big

2. _____ relating to women

3. _____ the part of your body where food goes first after you eat it

4. _____ relating to men

5. _____ a part of your body that receives, organizes, and sends information to other parts of your body

6. _____ the physical situation that someone or something is in

7. _____ with no bends or curves

8. _____ to cause harm to a person or animal

9. _____ to stay; to remain; to make stay or remain

10. _____ a part of your body that supports you and gives you shape

**C** Read the paragraph on animal adaptation. Work with a partner. What kind of animal adaptation is white fur? What is another example of animal adaptation? Write your example below.

Animal adaptations are changes to animals that help them to survive where they live. Some adaptations can be in how animals live or behave. Some adaptations can be in how they look. For example, animals that live in the Arctic often have white fur. The white fur helps them hide and be safe.

_____

_____

**D** Work with a partner and complete the Animal Adaptations Quiz. Then listen and check your answers. 🎧6.5

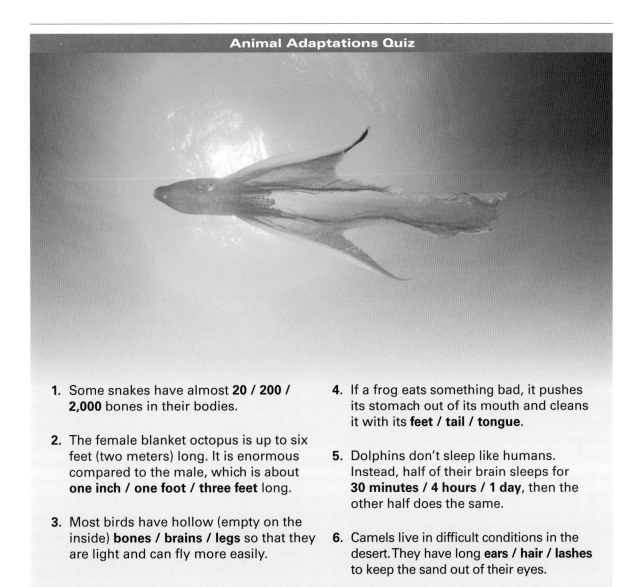

**Animal Adaptations Quiz**

1. Some snakes have almost **20 / 200 / 2,000** bones in their bodies.

2. The female blanket octopus is up to six feet (two meters) long. It is enormous compared to the male, which is about **one inch / one foot / three feet** long.

3. Most birds have hollow (empty on the inside) **bones / brains / legs** so that they are light and can fly more easily.

4. If a frog eats something bad, it pushes its stomach out of its mouth and cleans it with its **feet / tail / tongue**.

5. Dolphins don't sleep like humans. Instead, half of their brain sleeps for **30 minutes / 4 hours / 1 day**, then the other half does the same.

6. Camels live in difficult conditions in the desert. They have long **ears / hair / lashes** to keep the sand out of their eyes.

## CRITICAL THINKING  Categorize information

To categorize information means to put it into groups. Categorizing is a good way to deal with a lot of information. For example, animal adaptations can be put into two categories: *physical* (how they look) and *behavioral* (how they act).

REFLECT  Categorize information about adaptation.

You are going to hear more about animal adaptation. With a partner categorize the information in activity D into two groups: physical adaptation and behavioral adaptation. Think about the two categories as you listen to the next talk.

# LISTEN & SPEAK

## MORE THAN JUST A LONG NECK

---

**LISTENING SKILL  Take general notes—add details later**

When you listen to a talk, there is often not enough time to write detailed notes. Instead, you should write key words or phrases and use symbols. As soon as possible after the talk, you should re-read the key words in your notes to help you remember the content. You can add additional information to the notes, so they are more detailed.

Original notes: *insects' compound eyes - see all around*

More detailed notes: *insects' compound eyes = large / have thousands of lenses ➜ allows them to see all around, but picture not clear*

---

**A  APPLY** Listen to a talk about one type of giraffe. Take notes on key words and phrases. Then re-read your notes and make them more detailed. 🔊 6.6

**B  MAIN IDEAS** How has the giraffe adapted to the African savanna? Use your notes from activity A and check (✓) three items.

The giraffe's adaptations allow it to:

1.  ☐ keep cool.

2.  ☐ keep warm.

3.  ☐ eat leaves.

4.  ☐ stay safe.

5.  ☐ eat insects.

**C  PHRASES TO KNOW** Work with a partner. Complete the sentences with a phrase from the talk.

---

| hold up | look out for | get to |
|---------|--------------|--------|

---

1.  The giraffe's long neck allows it to _____ leaves high up in trees.

2.  The giraffe's long neck lets it _____ danger.

3.  The ligaments in the giraffe's neck allow it to _____ its neck.

**D  DETAILS** Listen again and look at the picture of the giraffe. Choose the correct word to complete sentences 1–8. 🔊 6.6

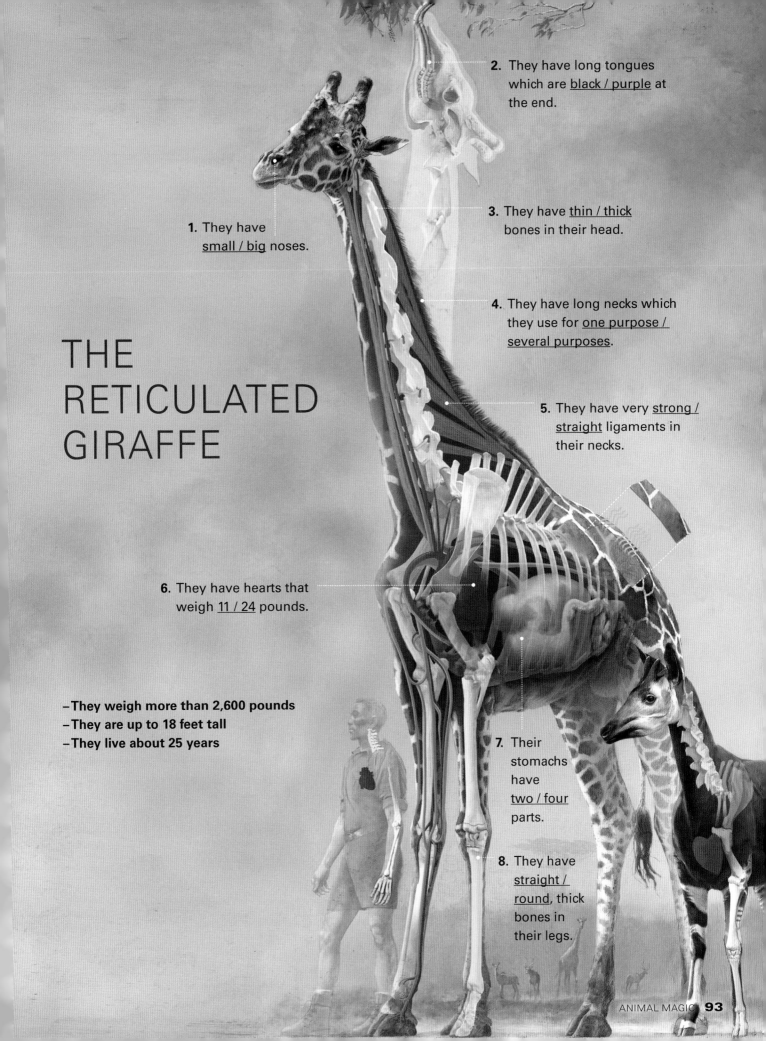

# THE RETICULATED GIRAFFE

1. They have <u>small / big</u> noses.

2. They have long tongues which are <u>black / purple</u> at the end.

3. They have <u>thin / thick</u> bones in their head.

4. They have long necks which they use for <u>one purpose / several purposes</u>.

5. They have very <u>strong / straight</u> ligaments in their necks.

6. They have hearts that weigh <u>11 / 24</u> pounds.

7. Their stomachs have <u>two / four</u> parts.

8. They have <u>straight / round</u>, thick bones in their legs.

- They weigh more than 2,600 pounds
- They are up to 18 feet tall
- They live about 25 years

You are going to give a presentation about how you adapt your behavior in the modern world. Use the ideas, vocabulary, and skills from the unit.

**E  MODEL** Listen to three students talking about how they adapt their behavior. Check (✓) the three things that they talk about. 🎧 6.7

Young people adapt their behavior to:

1. ☐ stay healthy.
2. ☐ earn money.
3. ☐ stay in touch with friends.
4. ☐ feel happy.
5. ☐ be good citizens.

---

**SPEAKING SKILL   Explain purpose**

Purpose is the reason for something. To explain the purpose of an action, you can use the infinitive with *to*.

> *I take shorter showers to save water.*

You can also use *help/allow* (+ person/thing) + infinitive with *to*.

> *The giraffe's long neck **helps it to reach** leaves in tall trees.*
> *It also **allows the giraffe to look out** for danger.*

You can also use *so that* + **subject** + verb.

> *The giraffe has a long neck **so that it can reach** leaves in tall trees.*

---

**F  APPLY** Listen again and complete the sentences. Write one word in each blank. 🎧 6.7

1. I use social media _____ _____ in touch with friends. It's the easiest way.

2. I call her or she calls me every week _____ _____ we stay in touch.

3. For example, I spend time in nature. That _____ _____ _____ feel happy.

4. If I don't have much time, I do a short run and I run fast. It _____ _____ _____ get a lot of exercise in a short time.

5. I usually swim for at least half an hour, and I swim fast _____ _____ I stay healthy.

**G** Complete the sentences with a purpose.

1. I go to the gym _____.

2. I listen to music _____.

3. I eat out in restaurants _____.

4. I'm studying English _____.

5. I use my computer _____.

6. I go to the doctor _____.

7. I call my parents _____.

8. I email my teacher _____.

---

## PRONUNCIATION  Saying structure words ⏵6.8

Structure words (such as pronouns, articles, and prepositions) often become shorter or change.

▸ Vowel sounds often change to the short sounds /ə/ or /ɪ/
  *a boy = /ə/ boy, night and day = night /ən/ day or night /n/ day*
▸ Sometimes a vowel or consonant sound is omitted
  *can = /kən/ or /kn/, want to = /wʌn tə/ or /wʌ nə/*

Notice the stressed **content words** and <u>reduced structure words</u>.

  ***I use social media*** <u>*to*</u> ***stay*** <u>*in*</u> ***touch*** <u>*with*</u> ***friends***.

---

**H PRONUNCIATION** Listen and underline the structure words that are reduced. Then listen again and repeat. ⏵6.9

1. I go <u>to the</u> dentist <u>to</u> keep <u>my</u> teeth <u>in</u> good condition.

2. I want to learn to speak confidently so that I can give presentations.

3. I check in on my elderly neighbor to make sure he's OK.

4. I take my own shopping bag to avoid using plastic bags.

**I PRONUNCIATION** Read the sentences aloud with a partner. Underline the structure words that are reduced. Listen and check. Then repeat. ⏵6.10

1. What do you do to be a good citizen?

2. I try to walk 10,000 steps a day to stay healthy.

3. I work as a taxi driver in the evenings to earn money.

4. My phone allows me to stay in touch with friends.

**J PLAN** Think about how and why you adapt in the modern world. Use the chart to help you.

| Adapt to . . . | How | Why |
|---|---|---|
| stay healthy | | |
| stay in touch with friends | | |
| feel happy | | |
| be a good citizen | | |
| other | | |

**K UNIT TASK** In a small group, discuss how you adapt your behavior. As you listen, take notes. How similar are your reasons and your partners'?

| Adapt to . . . | You: | Name: | Name: |
|---|---|---|---|
| stay healthy | | | |
| stay in touch with friends | | | |
| feel happy | | | |
| be a good citizen | | | |
| other | | | |

# REFLECT

**A** Check (✓) the Reflect activities you can do and the academic skills you can use.

☐ analyze differences between animals      ☐ take general notes—add details later

☐ relate ideas to your life      ☐ explain purpose

☐ categorize information about adaptation      ☐ adjectives and adverbs of manner

☐ give a presentation on how to adapt      ☐ categorize information

**B** Check (✓) the vocabulary words from the unit that you know. Circle words you still need to practice. Add any other words that you learned.

| NOUN | VERB | ADJECTIVE | ADVERB & OTHER |
|---|---|---|---|
| bone | focus | blind | clearly |
| brain | injure | enormous | easily |
| conditions | keep | female | unfortunately |
| degrees | notice | male | |
| stomach | | scared | |
| vision | | straight | |
| | | tiny | |

**C** Reflect on the ideas in the unit as you answer these questions.

1. How do you think you will you adapt your behavior in the future?

_____

_____

2. What ideas and skills in this unit will be most useful to you in the future?

_____

_____

# FIND YOUR PATH

A landscape artist maintains the many paths at the Great Garden of the Herrenhausen Palace in Hanover, Germany.

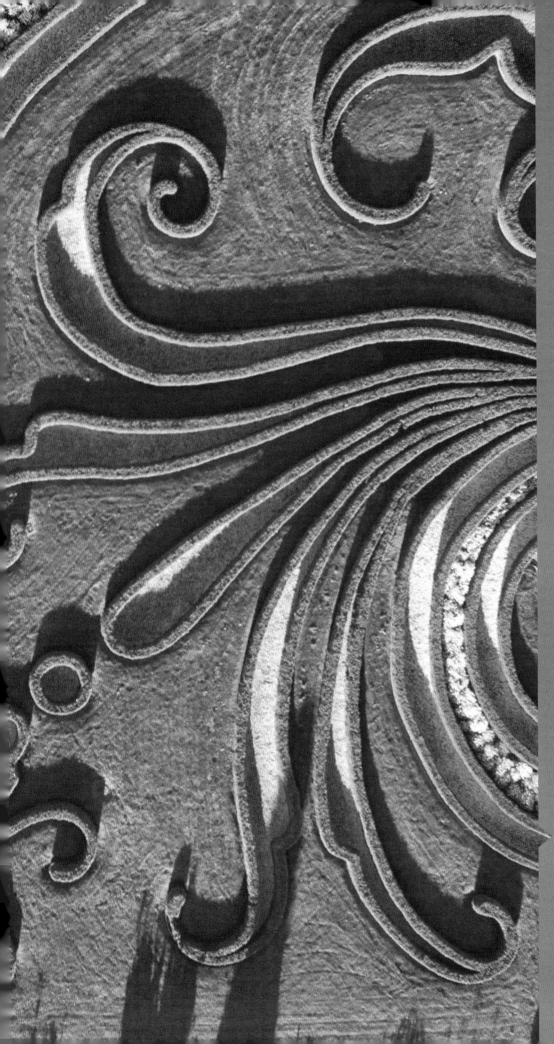

## CONNECT TO THE TOPIC

**1.** Would you like to have a job like the person in the photo?

**2.** Do you know anyone who has a job they love?

# PREPARE TO WATCH

**A ACTIVATE** How many words do you know for jobs? Make a list. Then compare your list with a partner.

_____

_____

**B VOCABULARY** Listen to the words. Complete the sentences with the correct form of the words. 🔊 7.1

| ancient (adj) | apply (v) | dream (n) | experience (n) | reach (v) |
|---|---|---|---|---|
| application (n) | complete (v) | expect (v) | goal (n) | step (n) |

1. Young children often have a(n) _____ of becoming a teacher, athlete, or doctor when they grow up. What did you hope to become when you were younger?

2. What is the best way to find a job: to ask friends and family for help, or to _____ for a job in writing?

3. Not many people _____ the top level in a company. Do you think you will get to that level one day?

4. Short term _____ like finishing an assignment can keep you motivated. Do you have any?

5. Most people hate to _____ forms. Do you hate to fill out forms, too?

6. The average person can _____ to change careers five to seven times in their lifetime. Do you think this is a lot?

7. Do you know what _____ you need to take to become a doctor?

8. In the past, job _____ were read by a person. Now a computer often reads them. Do you think this is good or bad?

9. An archaeologist tries to understand the _____ past by studying old ruins. Would you like this job?

10. You often need _____ to get a job. However, the only way to learn about the job is to actually do it. Is there a solution to this problem?

**C** Listen to two short conversations. Check (✓) the questions you hear answered. 🎧 7.2

Conversation 1:

a. ☐ Do you prefer to work on a project or stay at home?

b. ☐ Do you prefer to work alone or on a team?

c. ☐ Do you prefer talking to one person or talking to a team?

Conversation 2:

a. ☐ Would you prefer to be an archaeologist?

b. ☐ Would you prefer to be an astronaut?

c. ☐ Would you prefer to be an architect?

---

**SPEAKING SKILL  Ask follow-up questions**

When you ask a question and get an answer, don't let the conversation stop. Ask a follow-up question. A follow-up question is another question about the answer to the first question. Follow-up questions make the conversation more interesting and help you get more information.

> **A:** *Did you apply for the job?*
> **B:** *No.*
> **A:** *Why not?*

---

**D** Listen to the conversations in activity C again. Write the follow-up question used in each conversation. 🎧 7.2

Conversation 1:

**A:** When you're working on a project, do you prefer to work alone or on a team?

**B:** Oh, on a team, definitely.

**A:** Really? _____

**B:** I hate working alone. I get bored. I like to talk to other people.

Conversation 2:

**A:** But would you prefer a different job? Would you prefer to be an architect, for example?

**B:** Hmm . . . No, I don't think so.

**A:** _____

**B:** I'm not very good at drawing.

---

**REFLECT**  Consider your future path.

You are going to watch a video about someone who found her path or direction. Think about your own path. With a partner, choose three questions from activity B. Take turns asking and answering the questions. Remember to ask follow-up questions.

# FOLLOW
## YOUR OWN **PATH**

National Geographic
Explorer and archaeologist
Nora Shawki studies ancient
sites to learn about our past.

**A PREDICT** Look at the photo and read the caption. Discuss the questions with a partner.

▸ What kind of person becomes an archaeologist?

▸ What skills do you need to be good at this job?

**B MAIN IDEAS** Watch the video. Then choose the correct answers. ▶ 7.1

1. When did Nora decide to become an archaeologist?

   a. When she was nine years old

   b. When she went to London to study

   c. When she went back to Egypt

2. Why did Nora study a lot?

   a. Because she wanted to study in London

   b. Because she wanted to be an archaeologist

   c. Because she wanted to go back to her home country

3. Why did Nora go back to Egypt?

   a. To apply for grants and internships

   b. To get married and have children

   c. To study Egyptian archaeology

4. Which application was successful?

   a. The first one

   b. The last one

   c. None of them

**C PHRASES TO KNOW** Work with a partner. Discuss the meaning of these phrases from the video. Then take turns answering the questions.

1. When she returned to Egypt, how did Nora **move forward**?

2. How many of Nora's applications were **turned down**?

3. Why did Nora **keep trying** to reach her goal?

**D DETAILS** Watch the video again. Check (✓) the things that Nora says. ▶ 7.1

1. ☐ Egyptology is the study of ancient Egypt.

2. ☐ She studied to be an archaeologist in two different countries.

3. ☐ Some people told her that she should get married and have children.

4. ☐ Each application took two weeks to complete.

5. ☐ She expected the final application to be successful.

6. ☐ She thinks that if you follow your dream, it will be easy.

**E**  With a partner write three words or phrases to describe Nora. Then share your ideas with the class. Explain the reasons you chose them.

_____

_____

**F**  Listen to a person talk about reaching his goal. Complete the sentences with one, two, or three words. 🎧 7.3

1.  **A:** What is Ron's job?

    **B:** He's a wildlife photographer. He takes pictures of animals _____.

2.  **A:** When did he realize he wanted this job?

    **B:** At an _____ when he got a camera for his birthday.

3.  **A:** What was his first step to reach this goal?

    **B:** He _____ a lot. He took his camera with him everywhere.

4.  **A:** What was his next step?

    **B:** He went to college and studied _____.

5.  **A:** What problem did he have?

    **B:** When he left college, it was impossible _____.

6.  **A:** How did he move forward toward his goal?

    **B:** He worked part-time in _____ and took photographs in his free time.

A nature photographer gets especially close to an alpine marmot in Grossglockner, Austria.

## LISTENING SKILL    Listen for attitude

Speakers often use exaggeration to show their attitude about something. Exaggeration is when you describe something as much bigger than it really is. For example, Ron says:

*It was a **long and painful** couple of years.*

In reality, those couple of years were not longer than normal years. They also didn't really hurt. Ron is exaggerating. When you hear someone exaggerate, you often get an idea of their attitude. We can tell that Ron hated those years.

**G  APPLY** Work with a partner. Listen again and answer the questions. 🔼7.3

1. What is Ron's attitude toward the camera he got for his birthday?
   a. Positive
   b. Neutral
   c. Negative

2. What is Ron's attitude toward his college studies?
   a. Positive
   b. Neutral
   c. Negative

3. What is Ron's attitude toward life right after college?
   a. Positive
   b. Neutral
   c. Negative

**H  APPLY** Circle the words that Ron uses to show exaggeration.

1. I've still got the camera, but it's ancient now.
2. I took my camera with me everywhere.
3. I took millions of photos.
4. It was impossible to get work.

**REFLECT**    Talk about a goal you reached.

Work with a partner. Think of a goal you reached in your school or work life. Take turns asking and answering the questions. Ask follow-up questions if possible.

*What was your goal?*
*When did you realize that you wanted to reach it?*
*What steps did you take to reach it?*
*What problems did you have?*
*How did you solve the problems?*
*How did you feel when you reached your goal?*

# PREPARE TO LISTEN

**A VOCABULARY** Listen to the words. Complete the sentences with the correct form of the words. 🎧 7.4

| | | | | |
|---|---|---|---|---|
| contact (n) | interest (n) | opportunity (n) | salary (n) | unemployed (adj) |
| indoors (adv) | match (v) | respect (n) | skill (n) | uniform (n) |

1. If you are in a building—for example, a house or an office—you are

   _____.

2. Things that you want to learn about are your _____.

3. A(n) _____ is special clothes that you have to wear for work.

4. When you don't have a job, you are _____.

5. The fixed, regular money you earn from a job is your _____.

6. You feel _____ for someone when they are good at their job, or they are a good person.

7. If your work _____ what you love to do, you are happy.

8. The chance to do something that you want to do is a(n) _____.

9. The people that you know who can help you are your _____.

10. The things that you can do well are your _____.

**B PERSONALIZE** Choose the words that are true for you. Then compare your answers with a partner.

1. I would prefer a job where I work **indoors** / outside.

2. It's very / not very important to me to have a good **salary**.

3. It's important / not important to me that my job **matches** my **interests**.

4. As a child, I wanted / didn't want a job with a **uniform**.

5. In my life, I have had / haven't had a lot of **opportunities** to learn new things.

6. I think I have / don't have the right **skills** to be a teacher.

7. It's harder to find a new job when you are working **/ unemployed**.

8. I think / don't think it's important to get **respect** from my boss.

9. I have / don't have a lot of **contacts** in the world of business.

10. Working on a computer **matches / doesn't match** my personality.

**C** Work with a partner. Look at the infographic. Decide where you think these ideas should go on the infographic. Then listen and check your answers. 🔊 7.5

   a.  the people we work with show us respect

   b.  we are happy with our salary

   c.  we feel we are learning a lot

**We feel happy at work when...**

1    2    3    4    5    6    7

_____    _____    we feel important    we don't fear being unemployed    we have enough free time    we like the people we work with    _____

---

### CRITICAL THINKING   Use your imagination

Knowledge is important, but so is imagination. Imagination helps us to connect ideas and think of new possibilities. When you read or hear the results of research or a survey, try to imagine possible reasons for the results.

---

**REFLECT**   Look for reasons behind results.

You are going to hear an interview about finding the right job. Look at the information in activity C. With a partner discuss possible reasons for these results. For example, why does learning new things make us happy at work? Why is respect more important than money?

   **A:** *Why is learning at work so important?*

   **B:** *Maybe it's because people hate being bored.*

   **A:** *Maybe. Or it might be because . . .*

# HOW TO FIND THE RIGHT JOB

**A** Listen to an interview with a job coach (someone who helps you find a job) and take notes. Remember to write key words and add more detail later. 🎧 7.6

**B** **MAIN IDEAS** Work with a partner and compare your notes. Then complete the three steps to find the right job.

Step 1: Make three _____.

Step 2: Do some _____.

Step 3: Find _____.

**C** **DETAILS** Listen to the interview again. Choose a word or phrase to complete the summary. 🎧 7.6

| does that job | experience | help | interests | must-haves | online | skills |
| --- | --- | --- | --- | --- | --- | --- |

**Step 1:**

1. In list 1, write your _____.
2. In list 2, write your _____.
3. In list 3, write your _____.

Look for jobs that match the words on your list.

**Step 2:**

4. Do some _____ research.
5. Talk to someone who _____.

**Step 3:**

6. Write to companies and ask for their _____.

> **COMMUNICATION TIP**
>
> Use these phrases to ask for clarification when:
>
> - you don't understand.
>
>   *What do you mean?*
>
> - you want examples.
>
>   *What sort of things?*
>
> - you want to know how to do something.
>
>   *How do you do that?*

**D** Read the Communication Tip. Then listen and complete the conversations. 🎧 7.7

1.

**Tamara:** Your must-haves?

**Mahmoud:** Yes, the things that you must have in a job.

**Tamara:** _____

**Mahmoud:** For example, do you want to work indoors or outside?

2.

**Mahmoud:** The third step is to find opportunities.

**Tamara:** Find opportunities? _____

3.

**Mahmoud:** I mean don't wait for the right job to arrive. Go out and find it.

**Tamara:** _____

**Mahmoud:** Write to some companies and ask for their help.

**E** What do you think of Mahmoud's advice? Does he have good ideas? Will his ideas work for you? Discuss with a partner.

Shelton Johnson works as a park ranger at Yosemite National Park in California, USA. For this job, he wears a uniform and is outside most of the time.

You are going to interview a partner and help him or her find the perfect job. Your partner will do the same for you. Use the ideas, vocabulary, and skills from the unit.

**F MODEL** Listen to one student interview another student. Complete the lists. 🎧 7.8

| INTERESTS | SKILLS | MUST-HAVES |
|---|---|---|
| 1. _____ | 1. _____ | 1. _____ |
| _____ | _____ | _____ |
| 2. _____ | 2. _____ | 2. _____ |
| _____ | _____ | _____ |

**G** Compare your answers in activity F with a partner. Then listen again and check your answers. What job do you think the interviewer will suggest? 🎧 7.8

**GRAMMAR   Present perfect**

We use the present perfect to talk about past experiences when the exact past time is not important or not known.

  I **'ve been** to Rome. (the time is not important or not known)
  He**'s** already **taken** that course.

With a definite time in the past, we use the simple past.
  I **went** to Rome **last year**.

To form the present perfect, use *has/have* + (*not*) + past participle.
*Has* and *have* are often shortened to *'s* and *'ve*.

We often use *ever* in questions and *never* in the negative.
  **Have** you **ever used** that skill in a job?
  No. **I've never had** the chance.

**H GRAMMAR** Listen to excerpts from the conversation in activity F. Complete the sentences with two, three, or four words. 🎧 7.9

1. **A:** _____ to Egypt?

   **B:** No, I haven't, but _____ to Rome. I _____ there when I was 18.

2. **A:** _____ with children before?

   **B:** Yes, _____. I _____ in a summer camp a few years ago.

3. **A:** _____ a job that was inside?

   **B:** Yes, I have. I _____ a job in an office when I was 19.

**I GRAMMAR** Complete the conversations with the present perfect of the verbs. Use contractions when possible. Then ask and answer the questions with a partner.

1. **A:** Which countries _____ you _____ to? (be)

   **B:** I _____ to most countries in South America. (be)

2. **A:** _____ you ever _____ a summer job or a part-time job? (have)

   **B:** No, I _____. I _____ never _____ any kind of job. (have)

3. **A:** What skills _____ you _____ in this course? (learn)

   **B:** I _____ how to think more critically. (learn)

---

## PRONUNCIATION Connected speech 🔊7.10

When a word ends with a consonant sound and the next word begins with a vowel sound, the final consonant sound connects to the beginning of the next word. It sounds like the consonant begins the next word.

*That's a good idea.* ➔ *That's a good idea.*

When a word ends with a consonant sound and the next word begins with the same sound, we connect them. We say the consonant sound just once, but we hold it longer.

*A uniform makes getting ready easy.* ➔ *A uniform makes getting ready easy.*

---

**J PRONUNCIATION** Listen and notice how the sounds are connected. Then listen again and repeat. 🔊7.11

1. That's not a bad idea.
2. That question needs an answer.
3. My teacher really likes students to speak in class.
4. I think I have correct information.

**K PRONUNCIATION** Listen and write the sentences. Then work with a partner to mark the linking sounds. Listen again and repeat. 🔊7.12

1. _____

2. _____

3. _____

4. _____

**L UNIT TASK** Interview your partner and complete the lists. Write at least two words or phrases for each category. Ask follow-up questions. Then use the information to suggest the perfect job for your partner.

| INTERESTS | SKILLS | MUST-HAVES |
|---|---|---|
| 1. _____ _____ 2. _____ _____ | 1. _____ _____ 2. _____ _____ | 1. _____ _____ 2. _____ _____ |

Perfect job: _____

**M** Report back to the class on your interview. Listen to other students and complete the chart. Do you agree with the job suggestion for each person? What job would you recommend?

| Person's name | | | |
|---|---|---|---|
| Interests | | | |
| Skills | | | |
| Must-haves | | | |
| Perfect job | | | |

Artist Katherine Bernhardt works in her studio in Brooklyn, NY, USA.

# REFLECT

**A** Check (✓) the Reflect activities you can do and the academic skills you can use.

- ☐ consider your future path
- ☐ talk about a goal you reached
- ☐ look for reasons behind results
- ☐ discover your perfect job

- ☐ listen for attitude
- ☐ ask follow-up questions
- ☐ present perfect
- ☐ use your imagination

**B** Check (✓) the vocabulary words from the unit that you know. Circle words you still need to practice. Add any other words that you learned.

| NOUN | VERB | ADJECTIVE | ADVERB & OTHER |
|------|------|-----------|----------------|
| application | apply | ancient | indoors |
| contact | complete | unemployed | |
| dream | expect | | |
| experience | match | | |
| goal | reach | | |
| interest | | | |
| opportunity | | | |
| respect | | | |
| salary | | | |
| skill | | | |
| step | | | |
| uniform | | | |

**C** Reflect on the ideas in the unit as you answer the questions.

1. What have you learned about finding your perfect job?

   _____

   _____

2. What ideas and skills in this unit will be most useful to you in the future?

   _____

   _____

# THE HAPPY BRAIN

Children laughing,
Mongolia

## CONNECT TO THE TOPIC

1. Why do you think these children are happy?

2. When are you the happiest?

# PREPARE TO WATCH

**A ACTIVATE** How many verbs related to the brain and what we do with the brain can you think of? Make a list and then compare your list with a partner.

_____

_____

**B VOCABULARY** Listen to the words. Complete the sentences with the correct form of the words. 🔊 8.1

| basic (adj) | challenge (n) | diet (n) | look like (v phr) | produce (v) |
|---|---|---|---|---|
| cell (n) | deal with (v phr) | human (adj) | major (adj) | technique (n) |

1. The average adult brain has 100 billion _____. Each one can connect to tens of thousands of others.

2. A neurologist is a special doctor who _____ problems with the brain.

3. A good _____ for improving your vocabulary is keeping vocabulary note cards.

4. The _____ brain is 2 percent of a person's body weight, but it uses 25 percent of a person's energy.

5. There are many different parts to the brain and they are all necessary, but the three main or _____ parts are the cerebrum, the cerebellum, and the brain stem.

6. The size of your brain doesn't make a difference to intelligence. From photos taken in 1955, it _____ Albert Einstein's brain was a bit smaller than average, but he was much more intelligent than average.

7. The cerebellum is important for _____ activities like walking and moving.

8. As we get older, our brains get smaller. Eating good food is important. A good _____ can help slow down the changes in our brain.

9. Your brain _____ enough electricity to make a light bulb light up.

10. It's important to give your brain different _____, such as learning a language. Working the brain keeps it strong.

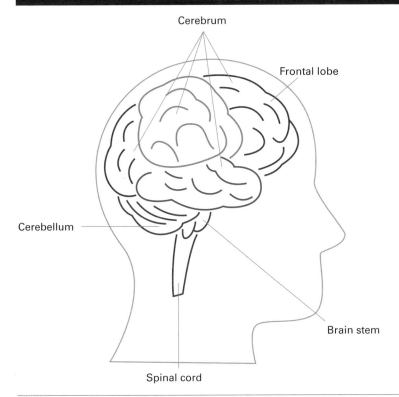

**The Human Brain**

Cerebrum

Frontal lobe

Cerebellum

Brain stem

Spinal cord

When you hear or read about facts, you can respond to the information in different ways.

*I already knew/didn't know that we have about 100 billion brain cells.*

*I was surprised to hear that the brain has three basic parts.*

**C** Look at the figure of the human brain. Then listen and match two facts to each part of the brain. Compare your answers with a partner. 🎧 8.2

1. _____ _____ the cerebrum

2. _____ _____ the cerebellum

3. _____ _____ the brain stem

    a. It deals with basic activities, such as breathing and your heart rate.

    b. It deals with moving activities, such as walking and standing.

    c. It deals with thinking activities, such as remembering and planning.

    d. It is about 4 percent of your brain.

    e. It is 11 percent of your brain, but it has 50 percent of the cells in your brain.

    f. It is about 85 percent of your brain.

**REFLECT** Discuss facts about the brain.

You are going to watch a video about the brain. Work with a partner. Read the Communication Tip. Then talk about the facts in activity B. What facts did you already know? What facts surprised you? Explain.

# WATCH & SPEAK

# DON'T YOU JUST **LOVE** THE **BRAIN?**

**A PREDICT** Look at the photo and read the caption. What do you think it means to have a love affair with the brain? Why do you think she feels that way?

**B MAIN IDEAS** Watch the video and check your predictions in activity A. Then read these statements. Check (✓) the statements that are true. ▶ 8.1

1. ☐ Marian Diamond thinks the human brain is amazing.
2. ☐ She has enjoyed studying the brain.
3. ☐ She is a student at the University of Berkeley.
4. ☐ She is interested in hats.
5. ☐ She is interested in how to improve your brain.

Marian Diamond has "a love affair with the brain."

**C PHRASES TO KNOW** Complete the sentences with a phrase from the video. One phrase is used twice in one sentence.

| There's no doubt | Nothing can compare with it | Take away |
| --- | --- | --- |

1. A full human brain that you can hold in one hand. _____
   _____ .

2. _____ the brain and you _____ the person.

3. _____ . If there's an opportunity to improve your brain, you want to be there.

**D** Which statement in activity C do you agree with most strongly? Tell a partner.

**E DETAILS** Watch the video again. Choose the correct answers. ▶8.1

1. How long has Marian Diamond spent studying the brain?
   a. 50 years
   b. 56 years
   c. More than 60 years
2. How popular is she on YouTube?
   a. She is the most popular college professor in the world.
   b. She is the second most popular college professor in the world.
   c. She is the least popular college professor in the world.
3. What did she publish a study about?
   a. The brain of Albert Einstein
   b. The life of Albert Einstein
   c. The thoughts of Albert Einstein
4. How many of the students have seen a human brain before?
   a. A lot of them
   b. About half of them
   c. Not many of them
5. What are the five items that are important to improve your brain?
   a. Diet, exercise, challenge, happiness, love
   b. Diet, friendship, change, newness, love
   c. Diet, exercise, challenge, newness, love

## SPEAKING SKILL   Ask questions to engage your audience

When you give a talk or a presentation, you can ask questions to keep your audience interested. Questions can be very helpful during the introduction to your talk. They get people to think about the topic and their experiences.

*How many of you have studied the brain?*

**F** **APPLY** Marian Diamond asked five questions in the introduction to her talk. Match the beginning of her questions to the end. Then listen and check your answers. 🎧 8.3

1. _____ How many of you have

2. _____ How many have studied

3. _____ How many have seen a

4. _____ Did you know that

5. _____ How many of you have heard

a. this is what you hope you look like inside?

b. about a cerebellum?

c. studied brains?

d. human brains?

e. human brain?

**G** **APPLY** Listen to the introduction to a talk. Complete each question with two or three words. Then compare answers with a partner. 🎧 8.4

Welcome. Today we are going to talk about challenge. ¹_____ challenge? Challenge is learning to do something that is new or difficult.

²_____ of you have challenges in your life right now? Almost everyone. Another question: ³_____ of you find those challenges difficult? Again, almost everyone. ⁴_____ that our brains need challenge? It's strange, but it's true. Our brains need challenge to improve. ⁵_____ that? It's because challenge actually changes our brain. "Use it or lose it." ⁶_____ of that phrase? Without challenge, we don't use our brain and it doesn't improve.

## PRONUNCIATION Intonation in questions 🔊8.5

Intonation is the rise and fall of your voice.

The voice often rises at the end of a *Yes/No* question.

*Have you heard of that phrase?*

The voice often falls at the end of a *Wh-* question.

*Why is that?*

**H PRONUNCIATION** Listen to the questions. Check (✓) the intonation you hear at the end of each question. 🎧8.6

|  | | Rising | Falling |
|---|---|:---:|:---:|
| 1. | Who here has heard of Marian Diamond? | ☐ | ☐ |
| 2. | Do you know why sleep is essential? | ☐ | ☐ |
| 3. | How does the brain produce ideas? | ☐ | ☐ |
| 4. | Is a good diet essential for a good brain? | ☐ | ☐ |
| 5. | Which university does she work for? | ☐ | ☐ |
| 6. | Do you want to improve your brain? | ☐ | ☐ |
| 7. | Can you draw a diagram of the brain? | ☐ | ☐ |
| 8. | What do you think is in this box? | ☐ | ☐ |

**I PRONUNCIATION** Listen again and repeat the questions. 🎧8.6

---

**REFLECT** Ask questions about the brain.

1. Work with a partner and choose a topic.

   ▸ love and the brain            ▸ newness and the brain

   ▸ exercise and the brain        ▸ diet and the brain

2. Write three questions to ask in the introduction to a presentation on that topic.

   _____

   _____

   _____

3. Ask your questions to another pair. Remember to use the correct intonation. Listen to their questions and try to answer them.

# PREPARE TO LISTEN

**A ACTIVATE** When you think of happiness, what activities do you think of? Work with a partner and make a list.

**B VOCABULARY** Listen to the words. Complete the definitions with the correct form of the words. 🎧 8.7

| | | | | |
|---|---|---|---|---|
| achieve (v) | concentrate (v) | depend on (v phr) | grateful (adj) | object (n) |
| calm (adj) | control (v) | explain (v) | luck (n) | work (v) |

1. A(n) _____ is a thing.

2. When you are _____, you don't show strong feelings or emotions.

3. When you _____ something, you have power over it and you can tell it what to do.

4. When an idea _____, it means the idea is a good one.

5. When you _____ a goal, you reach it after a lot of work.

6. When you feel _____, you are happy and feel thanks for something.

7. When you _____, you give information about something so that someone can understand.

8. _____ is when good things happen by chance and not by hard work.

9. When you _____ on something, you give all your attention to it.

10. When you _____ something or someone, you need them.

**C** Complete the sentences with the correct form of the words in activity B. Sometimes a word is used twice in a sentence. Then tell a partner if you agree with the statements.

1. I believe that the more I _____ in my life and the more successful I am, the happier I will be.

2. To be happy in life, you need good _____. If you have bad _____, things will go wrong and you won't be happy.

3. It's better to spend money on events, like a vacation, than on _____ like a new car.

4. I try not to _____ other people. They can disappoint you. I _____ myself.

5. When things go wrong, it helps if I stay _____ and don't get upset or angry.

6. It isn't possible to _____ what happiness is. You can only feel it.

7. You can't turn happiness on and off. You can't _____ it like that. It just happens.

8. If I feel sad, I don't try to make myself happy. That doesn't _____ for me. I just accept that I'm sad.

9. I listen to music when I'm studying. It helps me to _____ on my work.

10. I feel _____ for my friends. They make me happy.

---

**CRITICAL THINKING   Understand graphs**

To understand the information in a graph, follow these steps.

1. Read the title of the graph.
2. Read the labels on the x-axis (the horizontal line across the bottom) and the y-axis (the vertical line at the left side).
3. Look at the line going up and/or down in the graph.
4. Try to summarize what the graph is showing.

---

REFLECT    Read a graph about happiness.

You are going to hear a talk about happiness. Look at the graph and follow the steps in the Critical Thinking box. Then discuss the questions with a partner.

1. What is the graph about?

2. What is on the x-axis? What is on the y-axis?

3. What does the graph show? When are people happier? When are they less happy?

4. What reason can you give for this?

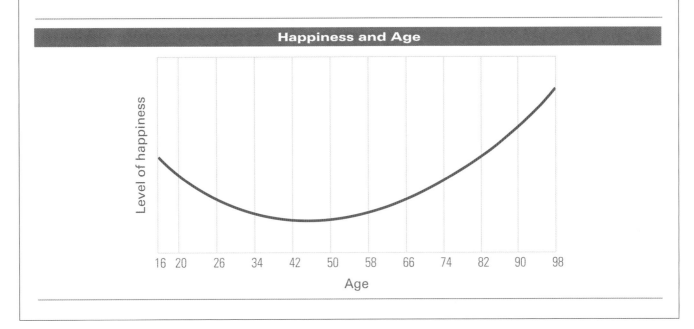

**Happiness and Age**

Level of happiness (y-axis)

Age (x-axis): 16  20  26  34  42  50  58  66  74  82  90  98

# LISTEN & SPEAK

# HOW TO BE HAPPY

This man in Tokyo, Japan, is happy at work.

**A** You are going to listen to a talk about three views on happiness. Listen and take notes. Remember to write key facts and use symbols. You can add details after the talk. 🎧 8.8

**B** **MAIN IDEAS** Use your notes to write a name from the box next to a statement. One statement is not needed.

| Sonja | The Stoics | Matt |
| --- | --- | --- |

1. _____ believed that you can only be happy if you are good.

2. _____ created an app to study happiness.

3. _____ believed that you can't teach happiness.

4. _____ wrote a book with 12 ways to become happy.

**C DETAILS** Listen again. Answer each question with two to four words. 🎧8.8

**Sonja**

1. What has scientific research proved about waiting for happiness?

   _____

2. If we want to be happy, which people should we give more attention to?

   _____

**The Stoics**

3. When did Stoicism begin?

   _____

4. What should you try to control?

   _____

**Matt**

5. What is the first question that Matt's app asks?

   _____

6. How often are we thinking about other things?

   _____

---

**LISTENING SKILL   Guess meaning from context**

When you listen, you will often hear words that you don't know. Don't worry! Try to guess the meaning of the words from the context (the words and sentences that come before and after).

*Scientific research proves that a promotion at work or a shiny, new object won't make us happy for long.*

The context tells us that *promotion* is a nice thing. It also tells us that a *promotion* is something that happens at work. With this information, we can guess that a *promotion* is getting a better job.

---

**D APPLY** Work with a partner. Listen to the sentences and guess the meaning of the words from the context. Write a definition. 🎧8.9

1. technique   _____

2. content   _____

3. wandering   _____

**E** Work with a partner and discuss the questions.

1. Who do you most agree with: Sonja, The Stoics, or Matt?

2. In her book, Sonja gives 12 techniques to achieve happiness. What do you think some of the other techniques are?

You are going to do a happiness experiment. You will try one of Sonja Lyubomirsky's techniques to achieve happiness. Then you will give a short presentation about your experiment. Use the ideas, vocabulary, and skills from the unit.

**F** Read three of Sonja's techniques to achieve happiness. Choose one for your happiness experiment. Do the experiment over the coming week.

**1. Practice being grateful—every day for one week.**

Write three things that you are grateful for. Choose things that happened to you that day. For example, write how you felt when someone smiled at you or when you ate good food.

**2. Practice being optimistic** (hopeful about the future)—**five minutes every day for one week.**

Imagine a time in the future (e.g., five years from now). Imagine that you are very happy and you have achieved your goals. Write about the details (e.g., what you do in your free time).

**3. Practice being kind—twice a day for one week.**

Do something nice for someone else. For example, tell someone why you like them or send someone a card.

**G MODEL** Listen to Alberto describe his experiment. Answer the questions. 🎧 8.10

1.   Which technique did Alberto choose? _____

2.   Why did he choose this technique? _____

3.   Does he think the technique works? _____

4.   What did he think about in his future? _____

5.   How often is he going to use the technique in the future? _____

6.   What other technique will he try? _____

**H NOTICE THE GRAMMAR** What two ways do Alberto and his classmate use to talk about the future? Underline the two future forms.

**Classmate:** Are you going to try the other techniques?

**Alberto:** I think I'll practice being grateful.

---

### GRAMMAR Future: *will* and *be going to*

To talk about the future, you can use *be going to* + verb or *will* + verb.

Use *be going to* + verb to talk about a plan for the future that you have already made.

    *I'm going to try the other techniques, too.*

Use *will/won't* + verb to talk about a plan you make while speaking. *Will* is often shortened to *'ll*.

    *I think I'll do it twice a week.*

You also use *will* for promises and offers.

    *I'll help you!*

To make a prediction about the future, you can use either *will* or *be going to*.

    *You're going to enjoy it. It'll be fun!*

---

**I GRAMMAR** Complete the conversations with *will* or *be going to* and the verb. Use contractions when possible. Then ask and answer the questions with a partner.

1. **A:** What _____ after this lesson? (do)

   **B:** I _____ a friend in a cafe. What about you? (meet)

2. **A:** What online courses _____ in the future? (take)

   **B:** I'm not sure. I think I _____ an online photography course. (do)

3. **A:** _____ a vacation in the next six months? (take)

   **B:** Yes, I _____ my grandparents in Canada. (visit)

4. **A:** What are your plans for the next 12 months?

   **B:** I _____ my studies and then look for a job. (finish)

5. **A:** Do you think that _____ a new language in the future? (learn)

   **B:** Yes, absolutely, but I _____ learning this year. I'm too busy! (not start)

6. **A:** What books _____ in the near future? (read)

   **B:** I think I _____ Sonja Lyubomirsky's book. It sounds interesting. (read)

**J** Complete the chart with information about your experiment.

| | |
|---|---|
| **TECHNIQUE**<br>Which technique did you choose? Why? | |
| **DETAILS**<br>What did you do? | |
| **RESULTS**<br>Did it work? How did you feel? | |
| **PLANS FOR THE FUTURE**<br>Will you use this technique in the future?<br>Will you try another technique? | |

**K  PLAN**  Use your notes in activity J to prepare your presentation. Include questions to engage your audience.

**L  PRACTICE**  Work in groups of three or four and practice giving your presentation. Use your notes to help you.

**M UNIT TASK**  Present the results of your experiment to another group. As you listen to your classmates, write notes in the chart. At the end, ask questions about their future plans.

| NAME | | | |
|---|---|---|---|
| TECHNIQUE | | | |
| DETAILS | | | |
| RESULTS | | | |
| PLANS FOR THE FUTURE | | | |

# REFLECT

**A** Check (✓) the Reflect activities you can do and the academic skills you can use.

☐ discuss facts about the brain

☐ ask questions about the brain

☐ read a graph about happiness

☐ present an experiment on happiness

☐ guess meaning from context

☐ ask questions to engage your audience

☐ future: *will* and *be going to*

☐ understand graphs

**B** Check (✓) the vocabulary words from the unit that you know. Circle words you still need to practice. Add any other words that you learned.

| NOUN | VERB | ADJECTIVE | ADVERB & OTHER |
|------|------|-----------|----------------|
| cell | achieve | basic | |
| challenge | concentrate | calm | |
| diet | control | grateful | |
| luck | deal with | human | |
| object | depend on | major | |
| technique | explain | | |
| | look like | | |
| | produce | | |
| | work | | |

**C** Reflect on the ideas in the unit as you answer the questions.

1. What activity did you enjoy the most in this unit?

_____

_____

2. What ideas or skills in this unit will be most useful to you in the future?

_____

_____

**Using a dictionary** Word stress

A dictionary tells you what syllable to stress (or emphasize) in a word. Most dictionaries show how many syllables there are in a word by using a dash (-) or a dot (•). They show the stress using a stress mark /'/ as part of the pronunciation guide for the word.

In the word *nature,* for example, there are two syllables. We stress the first syllable.

**na-ture** /'neɪ tʃər/ *n.*

**A**   Use a dictionary. Complete the chart with the words in the box.

| access | destroy | disadvantage | familiar | resident | variety |
|--------|---------|--------------|----------|----------|---------|

| Stress on the first syllable | Stress on the second syllable | Stress on the third syllable |
|------------------------------|-------------------------------|------------------------------|
|                              |                               |                              |

**Phrasal verbs** With *up*

A phrasal verb is a two- or three-word verb phrase. It always contains one verb and at least one other small word called a "particle." The meaning of some phrasal verbs is easy to guess—for example, *get up* means "to get out of bed." The meaning of other phrasal verbs is less obvious—for example, *show up* means "to arrive where someone is waiting." It's a good idea to learn these phrases the way you learn individual words.

**B**   Choose the best meaning of the phrasal verb in bold. Use context clues to help you.

1. I forgot the meaning of the word that I just **looked up** in the dictionary!

   a. moved one's eyes upwards      b. searched for information

2. Neighborhood meetings can sometimes **take up** a whole evening.

   a. fill or use time      b. lift higher

3. The class was difficult, but I studied hard and didn't **give up**.

   a. share something with someone      b. stop trying

4. Mountains **make up** a big part of the country.

   a. combine to form something      b. pretend something is true

5. He's very good at what he does. I'm glad he **moved up** in the company.

   a. get a more advanced job      b. go forward or higher

**Using a dictionary** Synonyms

Synonyms are words that are similar in meaning. The words *large* and *big* are synonyms. A dictionary may include synonyms in a box labeled *Thesaurus* or marked with the abbreviation *SYN*. You can also look for synonyms in a thesaurus.

THESAURUS
**trash** *n.* garbage, junk, rubbish, litter

**A** Use a dictionary. Match each word with the correct synonym.

1. argument (n) _____          a. usually

2. smart (adj) _____           b. fight

3. in general (phr) _____      c. intelligent

4. dangerous (adj) _____       d. job

5. careful (adj) _____         e. risky

6. chore (n) _____             f. cautious

**Phrasal verbs** With *get*

Remember: A phrasal verb is a two- or three-word verb phrase. It always contains one verb and at least one other small word called a "particle." It's useful to learn phrasal verbs in the same way as other new vocabulary. Here are some common phrasal verbs with *get*.

**get ahead:** to advance in a job; make more money
**get away:** to go on a trip
**get along with:** to be friendly with someone
**get around:** to move freely; go from place to place
**get back:** to return
**get by:** to have just enough of something, usually money

**B** Underline the phrasal verbs in these examples. Then complete the sentences with your own ideas.

1. To get along with someone, try to _____.

2. To get ahead at work, people need to _____.

3. When I get back home from school, I usually _____.

4. I think _____ is a great place to get away to.

5. I usually _____ to get around town.

**Using a dictionary** Choose the correct meaning

Many words have more than one meaning. In a dictionary, each word entry uses a numbered list to show the different definitions. For example, there are two main meanings for the noun *fan*. In Unit 3, *I'm a big fan*, the first definition is used.

**fan** /fæn/ *n.* **1** an admirer or person with a strong interest in a particular person or thing **2** a handheld or mechanical device that creates a current of air in order to cool

**A** Use a dictionary. For each word, find the best definition related to the topic of "music." Write the definition.

1. band (n) _____

2. note (n) _____

3. score (n) _____

4. gig (n) _____

5. staff (n) _____

**Prefix** *dis-*

A prefix is a group of letters that comes at the beginning of a word. You can add a prefix to a word to change its meaning. The prefix *dis-* can be added to some verbs, nouns, and adjectives to create words with opposite or negative meanings.

*dis-* + *organized* = **dis**organized, meaning "not organized, messy"

**B** Choose the best word to complete each sentence. Check your answers in a dictionary.

1. The sound of hip-hop music and classical is **dissimilar** / **disinterested** in many ways.

2. Some people **disconnect** / **dislike** rock music. They think it is too loud.

3. People often **disagree** / **dislike** about which kind of music is the best.

4. I think that not learning a musical instrument is a **disagreement** / **disadvantage**.

5. My phone is **disconnected** / **disliked** from the Internet. I can't stream music.

**Polysemy** Multiple-meaning words

Polysemy refers to a word that has two or more different meanings. Sometimes the meanings are similar but not exactly the same.

The noun *head,* for example, can mean "a person in charge" or "the body part above your neck." Sometimes one word can also be different parts of speech. The word *head* can also be a verb meaning to *lead.* Use context clues—the words before and after a word—to help you decide which is the correct meaning.

**A** **Choose the best meaning of the words in bold. Check your answers in a dictionary.**

1. Traffic on the highway was very **light**, so I got here fast!

   a. not weighing much              b. not having a great amount

2. The U.S. dollar and Japanese *yen* both **fell** to two-year lows on Friday.

   a. went down in value             b. moved to the ground

3. The movie was a **hit**—millions of people loved it!

   a. a success                      b. a strike with your hand

4. The **key** to success is hard work.

   a. a piece of metal that opens a lock    b. an important point

5. I **joined** a new book club. We meet every Wednesday evening.

   a. became a member                b. put something together

---

**Using a dictionary** Antonyms

Antonyms are words that are opposite in meaning. For example, an antonym of *pull* is *push.* The words *tall* and *short* are also antonyms.

Use a dictionary to find antonyms. Antonyms are often labeled *ANT* or *OPP*, meaning "opposite." They may be listed after a definition or in a *Thesaurus* box. You can also look for antonyms in a thesaurus.

THESAURUS
**pull** *v.* **1** to draw, tug, yank, jerk **ANT** to push

**B** **Use a dictionary. Match each word with the correct antonym.**

1. angry (adj) _____          a. different

2. rise (v) _____             b. heavy

3. light (adj) _____          c. new

4. similar (adj) _____        d. fall

5. old-fashioned (adj) _____  e. calm

6. loud (adj) _____           f. quiet

**Prefix** *trans-*

The prefix *trans-* can mean "across." To *transfer* something means "to move it from one place to another." *Trans-* can also mean "to change completely." For example, *translate* means "to change from one language to another."

When you see a new word beginning with *trans-*, you have a clue to help you understand the meaning.

**A** Complete each sentence with the correct form of a word from the box. Use a dictionary if necessary.

| transfer (v) | transition (v) | translate (v) | transparent (adj) | transport (v) |
|---|---|---|---|---|

1. I'm going to _____ from my low-paying job to a better one.

2. Many companies _____ their products to stores using trucks.

3. When you _____ "Abu Dhabi" from Arabic, it means "Father of the Gazelle."

4. You can see through a window because glass is _____.

5. I usually _____ money from my savings to my checking account to pay my bills.

**Collocations** *Waste* + noun and *waste* + *of* + noun

Collocations are two or more words that often go together. It's useful to learn collocations the way you learn an individual word. Here are some common collocations with the word *waste*.

waste (v)
**waste money**
**waste energy**
**waste time**
**waste resources**

waste (n)
**waste of money**
**waste of energy**
**waste of time**
**waste of resources**

**B** Underline the collocations in these examples. Then complete the sentences with your own ideas.

1. Buying new clothes is a waste of money.

   Buying _____ is a waste of money.

2. Playing video games is a waste of time.

   _____ is a waste of time.

3. It's a waste of resources to brush your teeth with the water running.

   It's a waste of resources to _____.

4. I try not to waste energy, so I turn off the lights when I leave a room.

   I try not to waste energy, so _____.

5. Sometimes I waste time by playing games on my phone.

   Sometimes I waste time by _____.

**Word roots** *vis* and *vid*

Many words in English come from Latin word roots. Knowing the meaning of Latin word roots can help you understand the meaning of unfamiliar vocabulary. The word roots *vis* and *vid* mean "seeing" and appear in many English words, for example: **vid**eo and **vis**it.

**A** Complete each sentence with the correct form of a word from the box. One word is extra. Check your answers in a dictionary.

| revise (v) | television (n) | video games (n) | visitor (n) | vision (n) | visuals (n) |
|---|---|---|---|---|---|

1. Hundreds of _____ came to the opening of the new zoo.

2. After talking to her instructor, she _____ her essay. The second draft was much better.

3. Nature shows about animals are very popular on _____.

4. My son is always playing _____ with his friends. Sometimes we don't see him for hours!

5. Sloths have very poor _____. They can't see very well at all.

**Base words and affixes**

A base word is a word that can't be broken into smaller words. For example, *fortune* is a base word. You can sometimes add affixes—suffixes or prefixes—to a base word to change its meaning or form.

**fortune** + **ate** = *fortunate*     **mis**+ **fortune** = *misfortune*   **un**+ **fortunate**+ **ly** = *unfortunately*

A dictionary will often list common affixes that you can add to a base word.

**B** Add the correct prefix or suffix from the box to each base word. Use a dictionary if necessary. Make sure any change is spelled correctly. Then write a brief explanation of each new word.

| -ably | -en | -ly | un- | up- | -y |
|---|---|---|---|---|---|

1. brain    *brainy    Brainy means smart.* _____

2. straight _____

3. notice _____

4. blind _____

5. keep _____

6. ease _____

**Suffixes** Change word forms

A suffix is a group of letters that comes at the end of a word. A suffix changes the form of a word. Some suffixes can change nouns or verbs into adjectives.

Common suffixes for adjectives are: *-able, -ed, -ful, -ic, -ing, -ish, -less*, and *-y.*

Words that end in *-ing* and *-ed* can be adjectives or verb forms. Use the context to decide if the word is an adjective or verb.

**A** Choose the correct adjective form(s) for each noun or verb. Use a dictionary if necessary.

1. interest     a. interesting     b. interestless     c. interestful

2. employ     a. employable     b. employed     c. employful

3. help     a. helpful     b. helpy     c. helpless

4. respect     a. respectic     b. respected     c. respectable

5. style     a. styleable     b. stylish     c. styleful

6. ease     a. easish     b. easy     c. easeful

7. comfort     a. comforty     b. comforting     c. comfortable

8. hero     a. heroful     b. heroing     c. heroic

**Prefixes** *in-, im-,* and *un-*

The prefixes *in-, im-,* and *un-* mean "not." You can add them to some adjectives to form new words with the opposite meaning. For example, *inexpensive* means "not expensive." Look in a dictionary to check for the correct spelling.

**B** Complete the sentences. Write *in-, im-,* or *un-* before each adjective. Use a dictionary if necessary.

1. His job application included some _____correct information.

2. The company would like to increase your salary, but it's _____possible. We don't have the budget.

3. She lost her job two months ago and has been _____employed since.

4. I like my colleagues, but the work is _____interesting.

5. Sorry, a 12:30 meeting is _____convenient for me. Can we change it to 2:30?

## Frayer model

You can better learn new words and phrases by using a Frayer model. A Frayer model is a graphic organizer that helps you describe a word in more detail than just a definition.

| **Defintion** | **Important Characteristics** |
|---|---|
| A diet is a weight loss program. | Avoid eating foods that cause weight gain<br>Usually focused on avoiding fats and sugars<br>Usually lasts for a few months or longer |
| **a diet** | |
| **Examples** | **Non-examples** |
| The Paleo diet, vegan diet, vegetaran diet, low-fat diet | Fatty foods, fast foods, candy, sodas |

**A** In your notebook, complete a Frayer model for the word *luck*.

## Homophones

Homophones are words that sound the same but have different spellings and meanings. For example, *meat* and *meet* sound the same, but *meat* refers to food and *meet* means "to join someone at a given location."

When you are listening to someone speak, use context to understand which meaning is correct. When you are reading, both the context and the spelling can help you.

**B** Choose the correct word to complete each sentence. Use a dictionary if necessary.

1. Drug companies **sell / cell** medicines.

2. Boys and men are **males / mails**.

3. People throw away a lot of food. There's so much **waste / waist**!

4. I usually **poor / pour** a little milk in my tea.

5. If you don't eat enough during the day, you may feel **week / weak**.

# VOCABULARY INDEX

*Academic words

# VOCABULARY INDEX

| Unit 5 | Page | CEFR |
|---|---|---|
| another | 69 | A2 |
| bank account | 69 | B1 |
| bill | 69 | A2 |
| borrow | 69 | A2 |
| can afford | 69 | B1 |
| collect | 69 | B1 |
| credit card | 69 | A1 |
| discount | 74 | A2 |
| extra | 74 | A2 |
| fee* | 69 | B1 |
| instead of | 74 | A2 |
| lend | 74 | A2 |
| likely | 74 | B1 |
| make | 69 | A1 |
| on sale | 74 | A2 |
| post | 69 | A2 |
| rent | 74 | A2 |
| skip* | 74 | B2 |
| transfer* | 74 | B1 |
| waste | 74 | B1 |

| Unit 6 | Page | CEFR |
|---|---|---|
| blind | 84 | B1 |
| bone | 90 | B1 |
| brain | 90 | A2 |
| clearly | 84 | A2 |
| conditions | 90 | B1 |
| degree | 84 | A2 |
| easily | 84 | A2 |
| enormous* | 90 | B1 |
| female | 90 | B1 |
| focus* | 84 | B2 |
| injure* | 90 | B1 |
| keep | 90 | A2 |
| male | 90 | B1 |
| notice | 84 | B1 |
| scared | 84 | B1 |
| stomach | 90 | A2 |
| straight | 90 | A2 |
| tiny | 84 | B1 |
| unfortunately | 84 | A2 |
| vision* | 84 | B2 |

| Unit 7 | Page | CEFR |
|---|---|---|
| ancient | 100 | B1 |
| application | 100 | B1 |
| apply | 100 | B1 |
| complete | 100 | A2 |
| contact* | 106 | A2 |
| dream | 100 | B1 |
| expect | 100 | B1 |
| experience | 100 | B1 |
| goal* | 100 | B1 |
| indoors | 106 | B1 |
| interest | 106 | B1 |
| match | 106 | A2 |
| opportunity | 106 | B1 |
| reach | 100 | B2 |
| respect | 106 | B1 |
| salary | 106 | B1 |
| skill | 106 | B1 |
| step | 100 | B1 |
| unemployed | 106 | B1 |
| uniform* | 106 | A2 |

| Unit 8 | Page | CEFR |
|---|---|---|
| achieve* | 122 | B1 |
| basic | 116 | B1 |
| calm | 122 | B1 |
| cell | 116 | B2 |
| challenge* | 116 | B1 |
| concentrate* | 122 | B1 |
| control | 122 | B1 |
| deal with | 116 | B1 |
| depend on | 122 | B1 |
| diet | 116 | B1 |
| explain | 122 | A2 |
| grateful | 122 | B1 |
| human | 116 | B1 |
| look like | 116 | B1 |
| luck | 122 | A2 |
| major* | 116 | B2 |
| object | 122 | B1 |
| produce | 116 | B1 |
| technique* | 116 | B1 |
| work | 122 | A2 |

# IRREGULAR VERB FORMS

| Base form | Simple past | Past participle | Base form | Simple past | Past participle |
|-----------|-------------|-----------------|-----------|-------------|-----------------|
| be | was, were | been | lay | laid | laid |
| beat | beat | beaten | lead | led | led |
| become | became | become | leave | left | left |
| begin | began | begun | lend | lent | lent |
| bend | bent | bent | let | let | let |
| bite | bit | bitten | lie | lay | lain |
| blow | blew | blown | light | lit/lighted | lit/lighted |
| break | broke | broken | lose | lost | lost |
| bring | brought | brought | make | made | made |
| build | built | built | mean | meant | meant |
| buy | bought | bought | meet | met | met |
| catch | caught | caught | pay | paid | paid |
| choose | chose | chosen | prove | proved | proved/proven |
| come | came | come | put | put | put |
| cost | cost | cost | quit | quit | quit |
| cut | cut | cut | read | read | read |
| dig | dug | dug | ride | rode | ridden |
| dive | dived/dove | dived | ring | rang | rung |
| do | did | done | rise | rose | risen |
| draw | drew | drawn | run | ran | run |
| drink | drank | drunk | say | said | said |
| drive | drove | driven | sit | sat | sat |
| eat | ate | eaten | sleep | slept | slept |
| fall | fell | fallen | slide | slid | slid |
| feed | fed | fed | speak | spoke | spoken |
| feel | felt | felt | spend | spent | spent |
| fight | fought | fought | spread | spread | spread |
| find | found | found | stand | stood | stood |
| fit | fit | fit/fitted | steal | stole | stolen |
| fly | flew | flown | stick | stuck | stuck |
| forget | forgot | forgotten | strike | struck | struck |
| forgive | forgave | forgiven | swear | swore | sworn |
| freeze | froze | frozen | sweep | swept | swept |
| get | got | got/gotten | swim | swam | swum |
| give | gave | given | take | took | taken |
| go | went | gone | teach | taught | taught |
| grow | grew | grown | tear | tore | torn |
| hang | hung | hung | tell | told | told |
| have | had | had | think | thought | thought |
| hear | heard | heard | throw | threw | thrown |
| hide | hid | hidden | understand | understood | understood |
| hit | hit | hit | upset | upset | upset |
| hold | held | held | wake | woke | woken |
| hurt | hurt | hurt | wear | wore | worn |
| keep | kept | kept | win | won | won |
| know | knew | known | write | wrote | written |

# PRONUNCIATION GUIDE

## SOUNDS & SYMBOLS

### Vowel sounds

1. **e**at, sl**ee**p /iʸ/
2. **i**t, s**i**p /ɪ/
3. l**a**te, r**ai**n /eʸ/
4. w**e**t, p**e**n /ɛ/
5. c**a**t, f**a**n /æ/
6. b**i**rd, t**u**rn /ɜr/
7. c**u**t, s**u**n /ʌ/
   **a**bout, b**e**fore /ə/ (schwa)
8. n**o**t, t**o**p /ɑ/
9. t**oo**, f**ew** /uʷ/
10. g**oo**d, sh**ou**ld /ʊ/
11. t**oe**, n**o** /oʷ/
12. s**aw**, w**a**lk /ɔ/

Dipthongs
13. f**i**ne, r**i**ce /ay/
14. **ou**t, n**ow** /aw/
15. b**oy**, j**oi**n /ɔy/

### Consonant sounds

1. **p**en /p/
2. **b**ag /b/

3. **t**ime /t/
4. **d**og /d/

5. **k**eep /k/
6. **g**et /g/

7. **f**eel /f/
8. **v**ery /v/

9. **th**in /θ/
10. **th**e /ð/

11. **s**ale /s/
12. ea**s**y, cau**s**e /z/
13. **sh**e /ʃ/
14. trea**s**ure /ʒ/
15. **ch**icken /tʃ/
16. **j**oin /dʒ/

17. **m**e /m/
18. **n**ot /n/
19. ri**ng** /ŋ/

20. **l**ose /l/
21. **r**ead, **wr**ite /r/

22. **w**in /w/
23. **y**ou /y/
24. **h**ome /h/

## COMMON TERMS

**syllable:** a unit of sound; one or more syllables make a word. A syllable in English has one vowel sound and 1-3 consonant sounds at the beginning or end.

> *book, re-flect, a-ca-de-mic*

**word stress:** the syllable in a word that is said more loudly and strongly

> *book, re-**flect**, a-ca-**de**-mic*

**sentence stress:** the words in a sentence that are said more loudly and strongly, usually content words (nouns, verbs, adjectives, adverbs)

> *I **stu**dy aca**de**mic **En**glish with Re**flect**.*

**focus word:** the most important word in a phrase or sentence; it usually provides new information and has the most stress. It is often the last word in a phrase or sentence.

> *I study **En**glish. I use a book called Re**flect**.*

**intonation:** the rise and fall of the voice (or pitch). Often our voice falls at the end of a sentence.

> *I **stu**dy aca**de**mic **En**glish with Re**flect**.↘*

# USEFUL PHRASES FOR CLASSROOM COMMUNICATION

## EXPRESS YOURSELF

### Express opinions

*I think...*          *In my opinion/view...*
*I believe...*        *Personally,...*
*I'm (not) sure...*   *To me,...*

### Express likes and dislikes

*I like...*    *I hate...*
*I prefer...*  *I really don't like...*
*I love...*    *I don't care for...*

### Give facts

*Studies show...*
*Researchers found...*
*The record shows...*

### Give tips or suggestions

*You/We should/shouldn't/could...*
*You/We ought to...*    *It's (not) a good idea to...*
*Let's...*              *Why don't we/you...*

### Agree with someone

*I agree. Absolutely.*
*True. Definitely*
*Good point. Right!*
*Exactly.*

### Disagree with someone

*I disagree.*
*I'm not so sure about that.*
*I don't know.*
*That's a good point, but I don't agree.*

## PARTICIPATE IN CLASSROOM DISCUSSIONS

### Check your understanding

*So are you saying that...?*
*So what you mean is...?*
*What do you mean?*
*Do you mean...?*
*I'm not sure what you mean.*

### Ask for repetition

*Could you say that again?*
*I'm sorry?*
*I didn't catch what you said.*
*I'm sorry. I missed that. What did you say?*
*Could you repeat that please?*

### Check others' understanding

*Does that make sense?*
*Do you understand?*
*Is that clear?*
*Do you have any questions?*

### Ask for opinions

*What do you think?*
*Do you have any thoughts?*
*What are your thoughts?*
*What's your opinion?*

### Take turns

*Can/May I say something?*
*Could I add something?*
*Your turn.*
*You go ahead.*

### Interrupt politely

*Excuse me.*
*Pardon me.*
*Forgive me for interrupting, but...*
*I hate to interrupt, but...*

### Make small talk

*What do you do? (job)*
*Can you believe this weather?*
*How about this weather?*
*What do you do in your free time?*
*What do you do for fun?*

### Show interest

*I see. Good for you.*
*Really? Seriously?*
*Um-hmm. No kidding!*
*Wow. And? (Then what?)*
*That's funny / amazing / incredible / awful!*

*Reflect* is designed to provide practice for standardized exams, such as IELTS and TOEFL. This book has many activities that focus on and practice skills and question types that are needed for test success.

| LISTENING • Key Skills | IELTS | TOEFL | Page(s) |
|---|---|---|---|
| Guess meaning from context | x | x | 125 |
| Listen for a speaker's attitude | x | x | 105 |
| Listen for gist or main ideas | x | x | 6, 13, 28, 45, 54, 60, 71, 77, 87, 92, 103, 108, 118, 124 |
| Listen for key details or examples | x | x | 7, 13, 23, 25, 28, 43, 52, 55, 61, 68, 77, 88, 103, 119 |
| Listen for numbers or time words | x | x | 13, 43, 45, 68 |
| Predict what you might hear | x | x | 10, 22, 28, 38, 44, 60, 68, 70, 77, 86, 103, 118 |
| Take notes | x | x | 7, 23, 45, 54, 60, 86, 92, 108, 124 |
| Understand causes and results | x | x | 55, 56, 107 |

| LISTENING • Common Question Types | IELTS | TOEFL | Page(s) |
|---|---|---|---|
| Check all the information that you hear | | x | 6, 87, 92, 101, 103, 118 |
| Complete a paragraph or summary | x | | 15, 28, 30, 39, 88, 101, 108, 109, 120 |
| Complete a table, chart, notes, or diagram | x | x | 24, 30, 62, 78, 92, 108, 110, |
| Complete sentences | x | | 13, 25, 39, 41, 45, 47, 53, 56, 71, 79, 87, 94, 104, 110, 125 |
| Match information to a category or person | x | x | 4, 7, 21, 36, 37, 60, 77, 91, 117, 124 |
| Multiple choice | x | x | 5, 13, 54, 103, 119 |
| Multiple response | x | x | 92, 94 |
| Short answer | x | | 14, 23, 45, 70, 71, 126 |

| SPEAKING • Key Skills | IELTS | TOEFL | Page(s) |
|---|---|---|---|
| Describe people or things | x | x | 25 |
| Express opinions about a topic | x | x | 15, 21, 43, 53, 61, 85, 89, 107, 109, 119, 125 |
| Give advice or suggestions | x | x | 31, 41, 78, 79, 80, 112 |
| Stress words and syllables | x | x | 40, 72, |
| Use questions | x | x | 120, 121 |

| SPEAKING • Common Topics | IELTS | TOEFL | Page(s) |
|---|---|---|---|
| Goals and future plans | x | x | 101, 105 |
| Money and spending | x | | 69, 71, 75, |
| Music and other kinds of entertainment | x | | 37, 39, 41, 43, 48 |
| Personal behavior and feelings | x | x | 96, 123, 128 |
| Science and nature | x | x | 57, 59, 64, 85, 89, 121 |
| Shopping and other hobbies | x | | 71, 73 |
| Work, jobs, and skills | x | x | 112 |
| Yourself, your family, or friends | x | | 20, 25, 26, 27, 29, 32, 71 |
| Countries, cities, and neighborhoods | x | x | 5, 9, 13, 15, 16 |

# CREDITS

**Illustration:** All illustrations are owned by © Cengage.

**Cover** Andy Vu/Adobe Stock; **2–3** (spread) © Juan Arredondo; **5** recep-bg/E+/Getty Images; **6** Atlantide Phototravel/The Image Bank Unreleased/Getty Images; **10** (tl) (tc) sansak/iStock/Getty Images, (tr) Peacefully7/iStock/Getty Images, (cl1) (c1) artisticco/iStock/Getty Images, (cr1) (cl2) VICTOR/DigitalVision Vectors/Getty Images, (c2) (cr2) Yutthaphan/iStock/Getty Images; **12** ansonmiao/E+/Getty Images; **14** RayR/Alamy Stock Photo; **18–19** (spread) © Annie Griffiths; **21** Leonid Plotkin/Alamy Stock Photo; **22** (t) Guy Levy/Bafta/Shutterstock.com, (bl) (bc1) (br) mayrum/iStock/Getty Images, (bc2) bsd555/iStock/Getty Images; **27** Brent Barnes/Shutterstock.com; **28–29** (spread) © "My Big Brother" 2014. USA. Directed by Jason Rayner; **34–35** (spread) © Allal Fadili; **38** Matej Leskovsek/Reuters; **40** Mark Bassett/Alamy Stock Photo; **42** Adam Hester/Tetra images/Getty Images; **44** Chad Batka/The New York Times/Redux; **50–51** (spread) © Igor Siwanowicz; **53** Hill Street Studios/Tetra images/Getty Images; **54** © Abelardo Morell, Courtesy the artist and Edwynn Houk Gallery, New York; **56** US National Library of Medicine/Pfizer; **58** Fairuz Mustaffa/Shutterstock.com; **60–61** (spread) CBS Photo Archive/CBS/Getty Images; **62** Kbailous/Shutterstock.com; **66–67** (spread) Eyevine Meng Tao Xinhua/Redux; **68** RgStudio/E+/Getty Images; **70–71** (spread) Stringer/Reuters; **76** © Jessica Wright; **78–79** (spread) fcafotodigital/E+/Getty Images; **82–83** (spread) Thomas Marent/Minden Pictures; **85** (bl) Jean-Louis Klein & Marie-Luce Hubert/Science Source, (br) RMfotografie/iStock/Getty Images; **86** © Remus Tiplea; **88** Joel Sartore/National Geographic Photo Ark/National Geographic Image Collection; **91** Stephen Frink/Stockbyte/Getty Images; **93** Fernando G. Baptista/National Geographic Image Collection; **96** track5/E+/Getty Images; **98–99** (spread) Julian Stratenschulte/DPA/Getty Images; **102** © Nora Shawki; **104** FotoFealing/Getty Images; **108–109** (spread) Max Whittaker/The New York Times/Redux; **112** Dina Litovsky/Redux; **114–115** (spread) © Mark Lehn; **118** © Luna Productions, "My Love Affair with the Brain"; **124** © Brian Doben; **126** Jacqueline Veissid/Getty Images.